eCOMMERCE: A PRACTICAL GUIDE TO THE LAW

To my children, Rachel, Rebecca, Ben, Jo and Sam whose uses and abuses of the Internet throw up many an interesting legal issue.

eCOMMERCE: A PRACTICAL GUIDE TO THE LAW

Revised edition

Susan Singleton, Singletons Solicitors

Published by
Gower Publishing Limited
Gower House
Croft Road
Aldershot
Hampshire GU11 3HR
England

Gower Publishing Company
Suite 420
101 Cherry Street
Burlington, VT 05401-4405
USA

Elizabeth Susan Singleton has asserted her right under the Copyright, Designs and Patents Act 1988 to be identified as the author of this work.

Revised edition 2003

British Library Cataloguing in Publication Data
Singleton, Elizabeth Susan
    eCommerce : a practical guide to the law. - New ed.
    1. Electronic commerce - Law and legislation   2. Electronic
    commerce - Law and legislation - Great Britain
    I. Title
    343.4'1'09944

Library of Congress Control Number: 2002106633

ISBN 0–566–08515–1

Typeset by Manton Typesetters, Louth, Lincolnshire and printed in Great Britain by TJ International Ltd, Padstow, Cornwall.

CONTENTS

TABLE OF STATUTES

Secondary legislation

International legislation

PREFACE

Preface to the revised edition

Since writing the first edition of this book almost two years ago, the speed with which new laws on ecommerce are produced by EU and UK Governments has not lessened. The Electronic Communications Act 2000 is in force. The ecommerce directive is about to be implemented and the first cases under the Data Protection Act 1998 are beginning to be decided by the courts. 2002 saw the EU jurisdiction regulation coming into effect, which has an impact, in particular, on sales via Websites and the distance selling directive has now been in force in the UK for nearly 18 months.

Changes on the horizon include a new EU data protection communications directive which may outlaw 'cookies' on Websites and change the law on unsolicited e-mails (spam). Spam is a practical problem for those using the Internet which has become worse over the last two years as more and more companies resort to unsolicited e-mails to drum up business.

What is clear, however, is that ecommerce is here to stay and brings huge benefits to businesses and individuals which far outweigh any legal risks. In fact most English laws apply equally well in cyberspace as to traditional methods of retailing or communication. There is little to fear and much to be gained. The areas of advice which my own clients require in this field vary widely from specialist advice on the competition or anti-trust implications of their contracts and arrangements to ownership of copyright or database right in works and software, from how to set up an e-mail policy for employees to what information needs to be included on privacy policies on Websites. Drafting contracts with Website designers, Internet software distribution agreements and services contracts where software is accessed on line (ASP arrangements) are frequent areas in which advice is sought. On the dispute side litigation is often over whether what a software licensor or designer provides is adequate and conforms to the contract or involves a dispute over ownership or copyright or infringement of a trade mark.

I have sought to concentrate in this book on those practical areas where advice is needed rather than legal areas which are not of importance or virtually never arise. Where possible I have given sources of further information, most of which is now free of charge on the Internet.

The aim of this book remains to advise readers of areas where law in the ecommerce sector might affect them and how they can best minimize that risk. Above all readers should seek to ensure they contract for ecommerce services or supplies on written or e-mailed terms. The 'back of an envelope', or even verbal contract, is one of the best sources of income for solicitors when people fall out later. Having the legal 'front end' sorted out reduces risk and reduces the risk of expensive legal action later. For example if all employees know where they stand at work as regards use of the Internet, such as where they have an e-mail policy like the one in the appendices to this book, it is easier to sack someone who has not complied, than to seek to terminate their employment where the rules were unclear and an unfair dismissal action may then result. Similarly commissioning a Website designer without contract terms stating who will own resulting copyright is silly. Including a sentence in an agreement making it clear which party owns the rights means a dispute is not likely to arise later on the point. Everyone knows where they stand.

Finally, the high profile demise of certain dot.com companies has not led to any diminution in the requirement for legal advice in the ecommerce field. Indeed more companies are using e-mail than ever before and most bigger companies have a Website, even if they have chosen not to buy and sell on line. Ecommerce looks as if it is here to stay. The law dates more in this field than any other. The book is up to date to 1 April 2002. However the law in this field dates quickly. The book does not provide substantive legal advice to readers, who should seek their own legal advice appropriate to their own businesses.

Preface to the first edition

Electronic commerce (ecommerce) has revolutionized the way many carry on business. It has grown from anarchic conditions with a laudable background of freedom of expression to being the principal means of communication between many businesses in the UK, their suppliers, customers, internally with colleagues, and externally with advisers. The 'new' uses require the application of laws to ensure a coherent framework for businesses. The growth in sales of goods and services over the Internet has meant that even more importance must be placed on the application of contract and related areas of law to ecommerce.

There are few specific electronic commerce laws in the UK. The government has brought out the Electronic Communications Act 2000, but this simply deals with the recognition of digital signatures. In any case, this largely duplicates the EU Electronic Signatures Directive (1999/93). The EU's Electronic Commerce Directive (2000/31) will by 17 January 2002 bring welcome harmonization to contract law as it applies to ecommerce throughout the EU. The EU's regulation on jurisdiction (44/2001) may help jurisdictional issues in the EU, but what is really required is coherent internationally agreed legislation such as already exists relating to areas such as intellectual property rights through bodies such as the World Intellectual Property Organization (WIPO, <http://www.wipo.org>) and domain name disputes through ICANN (Internet Corporation for Assigned Names and Numbers, the Internet standards body, <http://www.icann.org>) and others.

The difficulties the USA and EU have experienced in agreeing arrangements under the EU Data Protection Directive (95/46) for the transfer of personal data from the EU to the USA under their so-called 'Safe Harbor Agreement' (approved July 2000) have illustrated how difficult it is to reach international harmony in many of these areas. However, that has not stopped the massive growth of electronic commerce, nor should it. If the laws cannot keep pace, businesspeople will find ways to ameliorate the worst effects.

This book principally describes the law, rather than the technology and its phenomenal growth, but the April 2000 report of the UK's Oftel (Office of Telecommunications) and Office of Fair Trading, *Competition in e-commerce*, includes the following summary which speaks for itself:

> The pace of growth and take-up of e-commerce has outstripped every other technological development in recent times. Revenue from Internet sales in Europe in 1999 is expected to be $288 billion rising to $2 trillion by 2002 (KPMG Consulting November 1999). According to Datamonitor, UK consumers spent $60 million on-line last year, and are second in Europe only to the Germans for on-line shopping. E-commerce is becoming an important part of the retail business, but also offers advantages for business-to-business transactions. KPMG Research has shown that 4% of European corporate sales were transacted on the Internet – with 6% of corporate sales in the UK on-line. Projections suggest 14% of

business-to-business sales will be made on-line by
2003. (Oftel/OFT, April 2000, Chapter 2: <http://
www.oftel.gov.uk/superhwy/ecom0400.htm>)

Indeed, part of the aim of this book is to advise businesses on how to
minimize risk and maximize opportunities through ecommerce from a legal
perspective. For example, international law already largely recognizes
contract clauses specifying which laws apply to a contract. It is a simple
matter to state the relevant law on the Website concerned. Practical advice
rather than detailed legal analysis is given here.

The book is for both those who sell goods and services over the Internet,
and those who simply use e-mail, whether internally or externally. It provides guidance on information which should appear on Websites and what
are sensible rules on Internet use with employees. It is written by a practising Internet lawyer who every week is advising clients in the real world on
these matters. It includes details of the Consumer Protection (Distance
Selling) Regulations 2000, in force from 31 October 2000.

There is little point in describing in great detail English law, although the
writer is an English solicitor and where precise laws are described, they are
English law. Even Scots law can differ in material ways. General legal
guidance is given. For businesses moving into ecommerce, where a major
foreign market will be targeted, local legal advice from lawyers qualified in
that jurisdiction should be sought.

Electronic commerce presents major opportunities for businesses. The risks
can be overemphasized. Many other means of trading bear similar, if not
greater, risks. In practice, for most businesses the risk of loss of profit or
loss of reduction in overhead cost through not adopting ecommerce is
much greater than any minor legal risks which may exist. In some areas,
adopting ecommerce will be essential for business survival.

Few fields change as quickly as that of ecommerce. This book is up to date
to 1 February 2001. However, much of the practical advice will not date
quickly, and where possible references are given to sources of further
information. Website addresses are given for this purpose, even though they
may change and become out of date. They are often the easiest means of
finding the information. In any event, this book is not an alternative to
taking legal advice from qualified Internet/computer lawyers.

Finally, thanks are due to my husband, Martin, whose weekend childcare,
particularly of our toddler twin boys, made much of the writing possible,

which I juggle around the hugely increasing quantities of client work in the
ecommerce and commercial law fields. My many and varied clients in
ecommerce and other fields also prove a constant inspiration. There have
been 300 clients since I set up my practice in 1994, and rarely is a problem
straightforward. The real world is not like that. I learn from them on a
regular basis.

Susan Singleton
February 2001

Comments can be sent to the author at:

Singletons
The Ridge
South View Road
Pinner Hill
Pinner
Middlesex
HA5 3YD

Tel.: (+44) (0)20 8866 1934
Fax: (+44) (0)20 8429 9212
Email: <susan@singlelaw.com>
Website: <http://www.singlelaw.com>

1 EMPLOYMENT: E-MAIL AND THE INTERNET

Most firms using the Internet will have employee issues to consider. This chapter examines all the relevant issues and provides practical guidance for companies setting up an e-mail and Internet use policy. Examples of such policies appear in Appendices 1 and 2.

Use of the Internet at work

The Internet has made many employees much more efficient. It enables research to be undertaken well after normal business hours. It allows rapid access to a wealth of material. It saves time and money. In most cases, it is eminently desirable. However, it can also involve a major waste of time, and all employers need to decide what is an appropriate use of the Internet at work.

There are no right and wrong answers in this field. Some employers offer much more power and trust to employees than others. Largely, employment law allows employers to do pretty much what they like in laying down policies for what is permitted at work. Internet use may be banned, or it may be encouraged. Of course, there may be cases where an employee is dismissed for some relatively minor breach of their employment contract and the dismissal is found by an employment tribunal to be 'unfair', but in other cases where a major breach of the rules is found, then dismissal may be perfectly in order.

QUESTIONS

The following questions will help employers to determine the level of Internet use with which they are happy:

1. *Do we let employees make personal telephone calls at work?*
   If so, limited Internet use for personal reasons may be treated in a similar way. If not, then surfing the net for personal reasons may not be in accordance with the ethos or current rules of the company. However, if

the current policies refer only to use of office telephones for personal calls it may be hard to say this automatically extends to the Internet, so develop a clear policy covering Internet use. If local calls in due course become free of charge and an employee is surfing the Internet in their own time at lunchtime, then there may be less justification in refusing to allow them to do so on grounds of cost.

2. *Do all our employees need to use the Internet for their work?*
If not, there is unlikely to be any need to permit them to do so and the easiest way to avoid their wasting time on pointless searches is to deny them physical access to the Internet at work. If some do require access and others do not, then a clear policy saying who is, and who is not, allowed access should be drawn up.

3. *Do we want to encourage employees to become familiar with the Internet quickly, perhaps by allowing them access without restriction for personal and work-related matters, at least during an interim period which can be monitored?*
If yes, then unlimited use can be acceptable, particularly if the employees can be trusted not to abuse the access given. In other cases this could be disastrous, and output from employees could reduce substantially.

4. *Do we want to make a distinction between use of e-mail between our branch offices in the UK and abroad through our own intranet, and use and access to the Internet in general?*

5. *Do we expect to monitor the content of e-mails sent by employees at work?*
This is normally lawful if the employees are told, otherwise data protection and human rights legislation may be breached. The Telecommunications Lawful Business Practice (Interception of Communications) Regulations 2000 (SI 2000/2699) came into force on 24 October 2000 under the Regulation of Investigatory Powers Act 2000 (RIP Act), which are also relevant in this area. They permit interception for most business purposes without employee consent. Many telephone calls are recorded at work, particularly those of telesales staff in call centres and employees taking telephone orders of shares and other securities.

An e-mail policy which can be used in practice is set out in Appendix 1.

Legal issues

Employees need to be treated without discrimination in accordance with the law. Employers in the UK which breach the employment contract may find they are guilty of constructive dismissal, and may face a claim for damages of up to £50,000 (the current maximum level, although an unlimited amount can be claimed for provable loss where race or sex discrimination is found) for unfair dismissal and any additional damages for breach of contract.

Employment issues must therefore be treated very carefully indeed in this field. If employees know the rules to which they are subject and they break them, it is much easier for the employer to take action within the law and without incurring liability.

CASE EXAMPLE

LJ. Franchi v. Focus Management Consultants Ltd (14 June 1999, Liverpool Employment Tribunal, Case no. 2102862/98)

Facts   Mrs Franchi was personal assistant to the managing director of Focus, a small management consultancy firm, in Liverpool. She worked for the company for two years before notifying her boss that she was pregnant. The company set up an 'honesty box' for employees to pay for personal telephone calls. Mrs Franchi did not follow the new arrangement, and had to attend a disciplinary hearing. She was given a written warning after admitting she knew about the box, and was told she would be sacked for future breaches.

Several weeks later her boss found that (1) in working hours (that is, not during her work breaks) and (2) without consent of the employer, she had been accessing the Internet extensively to arrange a holiday. She had made 150 searches over a four-day period.

Her boss tackled her over this. She said she had just used the Internet once in her lunch break. The company suspended her. At her disciplinary hearing she said she had never been told not to make personal use of the Internet and telephone at work. She was sacked. She said this was because of her pregnancy. The company said it was for misconduct.

The matter went to a Liverpool employment tribunal.

Findings

1 The tribunal held by two to one that she was not unfairly dismissed. Focus were right to sack her for misconduct, and as a senior employee she should have known not to make personal calls at work. In any event, she had received the warning letter.

2 However, she should have been given a month's notice, as the actions she had taken were not enough to justify dismissal without notice. She was entitled to a month's pay in lieu of notice.

Lessons   The lessons from this case are that employers should have a clear Internet policy so that employees cannot argue that they were unaware of the rules. There was a risk here that the tribunal might have found against Focus, as there were no clear rules in place.

The fact that Mrs Franchi had already been given a written warning helped Focus. Making sure that proper procedures are followed reduces the risk of company liability later.

What is reasonable use of the Internet at work?

If an employee policy is in place, then employees will know what is permitted and what is not. For example, they may be banned entirely from using the Internet at work. In the policy given in Appendix 2, some use is allowed but is limited to lunch and other breaks. It is not allowed before and after work, when employees are less likely to be supervised. An employee staying on at work for three hours using company heat and light for extensive personal Internet searches is making unreasonable use of company property, whereas a ten-minute Internet search at work on a personal matter in the lunch break may avoid an employee departing for an extensive one-hour-plus shopping trip, and may actually save the employer money.

If there is a written policy, make sure that all employees, including new employees, are sent a copy and told about it verbally or by e-mail when they join the firm. In her legal practice, the author has frequently come across clients in all sectors who have internal policies which are well drafted and would ensure compliance with the law, but which are not sent to all employees or not read by employees, and are disregarded. Some employees may not know the policy exists. It is sensible to include a description of the policy as part of the induction process for new employees.

If the employer has not drawn the policy to the attention of the employee, then it will not apply. The terms are unlikely to be part of the employee's conditions of employment if they are not drawn to the employee's attention or clearly sent to them. The employee may breach the policy but not be in breach of their employment contract if this occurs.

Make sure external contractors are also shown the policy, or relevant parts of it. There should be a separate written contract with such people or the agency which employs them, and the policy could be attached. Many businesses use self-employed contractors and need to make sure they are as aware of the rules as anyone else. Many of the customers or suppliers who deal with the company will have no idea whether a particular individual is working at the company as an employee or on a self-employed basis.

What is 'reasonable' in this area should be determined by the employer through a conscious decision-making process. It is not sensible to rely on individuals' personal moral codes. Some will think it acceptable, for example, to 'steal' stationery from work, use office stamps or make personal international telephone calls. Others will offer to pay for every 10p personal call. Employees need rules so that everyone knows where they stand. A company without policies in this area is at risk of employees citing in their defence other employees who have 'got away with it' or whose conduct has been ignored or tacitly sanctioned.

What is reasonable may depend on the business concerned. Staff employed at a call centre to take telephone calls all day may not be expected ever to have time for personal telephone calls, whereas in many offices it is accepted that individuals doing normal office work will be making doctor's appointments and arranging holidays at work, at least by telephone, although preferably during their official breaks.

Employer liability

For most areas of law, the employer is legally liable or responsible for breaches of the law by employees. This may not seem fair, particularly if the employer has gone out of its way to tell employees what is forbidden, and the employee, in deliberately breaching the rule, then causes the employer to be liable for damages, but this is what legislation and case law provides.

A 'FROLIC OF THEIR OWN'

It is only where the employee is clearly on a 'frolic of their own' (as some cases have described it) that the employer can avoid liability. Employee–employer cases where this is the case usually only arise where the employee is doing something entirely unrelated to work. For example, an employee may murder someone at work. This is not murder by the employer. However, if a ship the company has built is defective and passengers are drowned, the company – or indeed the directors – may be liable for corporate manslaughter. The difference depends on whether the action was part of the work/job or not.

Other examples have included employees entering into restrictive arrangements with competitors in breach of UK competition law and against company instructions. The cartel activities were unknown to the directors and in breach of company policies. The company was still liable (*DGFT* v. *Pioneer Concrete Ltd* [1995] Tr LR 355 (HL)).

Defamation

The Defamation Act 1996 imposes liability for libel and slander (untrue statements which damage someone's reputation). Many employers are worried about liability for defamation caused by employee statements made by e-mail. Of course, e-mail is no more risky than telephone and paper messages in this field, and there are no special laws in this area, although the liability of Internet Service Providers is addressed in the EU Electronic Commerce Directive (2000/31, 8 June 2000, OJ L178/1, 17 July 2000) (see below).

However, employees may feel freer to express themselves in casual language than with other media, and should be encouraged to think carefully about its content before they send an e-mail. They also need to be told to exercise caution when 'cc-ing' or copying e-mails to third parties. This can be done by accident and result in disclosure of company confidential information to the wrong person.

ISPS AND DEFAMATION: EU ELECTRONIC COMMERCE DIRECTIVE

Article 14 of Directive 2000/31 states that the Internet Service Provider (ISP) will not be liable, unless a court injunction orders otherwise, for the information stored, on condition that:

> (a) *the provider does not have actual knowledge of illegal activity or information that the activity is illegal and, as regards claims for damages, is not aware of facts or circumstances from which illegal activity or information is apparent; or*
>
> (b) *the provider, upon obtaining such knowledge or awareness, acts expeditiously to remove or to disable access to the information.*

Nor must EU member states impose any obligation on ISPs to monitor content (Article 15). These provisions apply where the 'information society service is provided that consists in the storage of information provided by a recipient of the service'. Article 12 describes the ISP as simply a 'mere conduit' as long as it does not initiate the transmission, does not select the receiver of the transmission, and does not select or modify the information contained in the transmission.

The provisions of the Electronic Commerce Directive, when in force (it must be implemented by 17 January 2002 although the UK is to implement it late in 2002), will not, however, help employers avoid liability, as the employer is responsible for the employee's actions and would not be regarded as a separate external service provider of Internet services used by the employee.

CASE EXAMPLE

Laurence Godfrey v. Demon Internet Ltd **(April 1999, High Court, and April 2000, settlement)**

The Facts Someone sent a squalid and defamatory posting to a US Demon newsgroup, as if it had come from a Dr Godfrey. Dr Godfrey became aware of the e-mail which defamed him. He required Demon, the ISP, to remove it. It did not immediately do so. The message remained there for ten days, and was only removed through the normal removal procedures applicable to all messages. He sued Demon for defamation.

Findings The High Court held that Demon was liable. It was unable to prove that it did not 'know or have reason to believe that' what it did contributed to the publication of a defamatory statement under the 1996 Act. It appealed, but after Demon was purchased by a new owner, it settled with Dr Godfrey, by payment of £15,000 and legal costs (estimated at £250,000).

Lessons ISPs are advised to remove offending material as soon as it is brought to their attention, as in practice they have no axe to grind in arguing over whether the material of which complaint is made does indeed libel someone or breach copyright. The removal of allegedly illegal material may lead to an action such as that brought in April 2000 in the wake of the *Godfrey* decision when an ISP required a gay magazine, *Pink Paper*, to close its Website after complaint from a journal in the same sector that material defamed it. *Pink Paper* has launched an action under European human rights law.

Monitoring employee e-mails and calls

If employers are liable for the calls and e-mails of employees which may be libellous, the employer needs to do more than trust most employees. A monitoring system is a good idea. However, this depends very much on the atmosphere and ethos of the company concerned. Some have a corporate culture which could not withstand such 'snooping'. Employees might leave if this took place. Others would expect it. Always weigh up the effect on staff morale and staff retention policies before making any change which may cause employee problems. In practice, this can be even more important than legal issues. In sectors where staff are very hard to recruit, stringent e-mail policies and what might be seen as infringement of personal liberties could lead to an exodus of key people. In other industries, where workers are delighted to be in work at all, a rather strict e-mail policy would not cause problems. The Regulations (SI 2000/2699), mentioned above permit such monitors, although compliance with the Data Protection Act 1998 Code of Practice in 'The use of personal data Employer/Employee Relationships' (Draft October 2000) is also necessary (see: <http://www.dataprotection.gov.uk>).

In unionized companies, it may be necessary to discuss such a change with the union before it is instituted.

Many employers have monitored employee telephone calls for many years. Most employees who take share purchase or sale orders over the telephone expect calls to be recorded. Staff in call centres know that random calls are recorded to assess whether the staff are following the rules on what is said to callers on the telephone, or whether callers are given rude, unhelpful advice.

E-MAIL AND MONITORING OF EMPLOYEE E-MAIL

Data Protection Employment Code
The Data Protection Act 1998 Code of Practice *The use of personal data – employer/employee relationships* (Draft issued October 2000) makes it clear that compliance with the Telecommunications (Lawful Business Practice) (Interception of Communications) Regulations 2000 (SI 2000/2699) (which allow interception for a wide range of reasons – see below) will not necessarily ensure compliance with the data protection legislation. The Information Commissioner will take into account the extent to which an employer has complied with the Code when determining whether there has been a breach of the Principles and, if there has, whether formal action is appropriate. On email and internet issues the Code says that there is no Data Protection provision that requires an employer to allow employees to use the employer's telephone system, e-mail system or Internet access for personal communications. Monitoring of business communications might also intrude on an employee's privacy or autonomy to the extent that personal data are processed unfairly. For example, employees might well want to impart personal information by telephone or e-mail for business reasons which they only want to be revealed to the intended recipients, such as, personal reasons for asking for a meeting to be postponed. They may also have legitimate concerns

about constraints on their autonomy at work. The extent to which these are justified may depend on the nature of the work but routine monitoring of the content of all communications sent and received at work is in many cases likely to go too far, the Code says.

The Guidance then provides some standards for monitoring of communications covering matters such as letting employees know what will and will not be read, of their e-mails at work. There is also a section on telephone monitoring. Advice on e-mails includes 'If it is necessary to check the mail boxes of employees in their absence make sure they are aware this will happen. The purpose of such monitoring is to ensure the business responds properly to its customers and other contacts. Only use the information for this purpose unless it reveals criminal offences or gross misconduct. Do not open e-mails that are clearly personal'. 'Provide a means by which employees can effectively expunge from the system e-mails they receive or send'. If the employee is not allowed to send personal e-mails at work, presumably this requirement would not have to be imposed.

The Code is on the Internet at www.dataprotection.gov.uk under Codes of Practice.

Human Rights Act 1998
Since 2 October 2000 the Human Rights Act 1998 has ensured privacy rights under the law. Article 8 of Schedule 1 of the Act provides that 'everyone has the right to respect for his private and family life, his home and his correspondence'. The writer's view is that if an employer prohibits use of its computers for personal purposes then it is hardly the employer's fault if it reads a very personal e-mail of the employee. The employee complaining about breach of human rights would not, in legal parlance, be coming to the court with 'clean hands' and is unlikely to have much recourse. Employers however should ensure they act fairly and sensibly and if a very personal employee e-mail is found it should obviously not be disseminated widely by the employer.

Regulation of Investigatory Powers Act 2000
The Regulation of Investigatory Powers Act 2000 received royal assent on 28 July 2000. The relevant part of the Act came into force on 24 October 2000 by SI 2000/2699. The Telecommunications Data Protection Directive requires member states to protect the confidentiality of communications made by means of a public telecommunications network. The Regulation of Investigatory Powers Act 2000 repealed the 1985 Act and provided a new regime to govern interception and protect confidentiality.

The directive allows member states to authorize interception of communications to provide evidence of commercial transactions or other business communications, for national security, to deduct crime and to detect unauthorized use of telecommunications systems. Therefore, the government made the Telecommunications Lawful Business Practice (Interception of Communications) Regulations 2000 (SI 2000/2699) under Section 4(2) of the RIP Act, to specify the circumstances in which both private businesses and public authorities may lawfully intercept communications.

Lawful Business Practice Regulations
The Telecommunications Lawful Business Practice (Interception of Communications) Regulations came into force on 24 October 2000. The regulations allow businesses and public authorities to intercept communications for a range of purposes without consent. They also allow certain charities to monitor (but not record) calls made to their helplines. The regulations cover all types of communication over a public network, including, for example, fax and e-mail.

The regulations authorize the following interception activities:

a monitoring or recording of business communications by businesses or public authorities in order to provide evidence of the communications for the purpose of either establishing the existence of facts or ascertaining compliance with practices or procedures. (This allows businesses and public authorities to intercept communications without consent for purposes such as: providing evidence of a commercial transaction; providing evidence of other business communications to establish facts or ascertain compliance with regulatory practices or procedures; audit; debt recovery, and dispute-resolution.)
b monitoring or recording of business communications by businesses or public authorities for the purpose of detecting and preventing crime or detecting the unauthorized use of a telecoms system. (This allows businesses and public authorities to intercept communications without consent for purposes such as: preventing or detecting crime; detecting the unauthorized use of an electronic communications system; protecting a network against viruses or hackers, and combatting or investigating fraud or corruption.)
c monitoring or recording of business communications by public authorities in the interests of national security.
d monitoring (but not recording) of communications to helplines providing confidential counselling and support services free of charge on an anonymous basis. (This allows charitable bodies to provide immediate

support and protection to front-line staff who provide counselling advice to the public.)

If businesses wish to intercept communications for purposes outside the scope of the regulations, they need (as required by Section 3(1) of the RIP Act), to have reasonable grounds to believe that callers had consented to the interception. The government says that while the RIP Act and these regulations govern the lawful interception of communications, they in no way prejudice the rules on the processing of personal data laid out in the Data Protection Act 1998. If businesses obtain personal data as the result of an interception authorized under the RIP Act or the lawful business practice Regulations, they will need to ensure that any subsequent use or processing of that information complies with the principles of data protection established in the Data Protection Act (see Data Protection Code (pg. 9)).

CASE EXAMPLES: SACKINGS FOR E-MAIL ABUSE

Recent examples include the Dow Chemical Company, which found that employees at all levels had sent pornography and violent images from company computers, leading to the firing of 50 workers and the disciplining of 200 others in July 2000.

In 1999, the *New York Times* sacked 22 employees in Virginia, USA, for passing around potentially offensive e-mails.

Xerox fired 40 workers for spending work time (sometimes up to eight hours a day) surfing pornographic and shopping sites on the Web.

In September 2000 it was announced that the UK telecommunications company Orange had sacked 45 employees in call centres in Darlington, Peterborough and Hertfordshire for distributing to colleagues pornography from the Internet in breach of company rules. The company rules prohibit the creation and exchange of messages which are 'offensive, harassing, obscene, racist, sexist, threatening or libellous'.

Increasingly, employment tribunals are hearing disputes relating to sexual harassment by e-mail and unfair dismissal for alleged personal use of the Internet.

Other relevant new legislation will be the Freedom of Information Act 2000 (accessible on the same Website as the Electronic Communications Act 2000), but that principally relates to access by individuals to personal information held about them by governmental and quasi-governmental bodies.

ADVICE TO EMPLOYERS

Employers need to know what e-mails employees are sending at work. The e-mails can bind the company to contracts in law. They can lead the company into liability for substantial damages for breach of legislation such as the Defamation Act 1996, and Copyright, Designs and Patents Act 1988. It is normal practice for junior employees to have their letters checked and approved by their boss. E-mail should be no different.

If e-mails are allowed to be sent for private purposes at work, there may be a privacy issue under the Data Protection Act 1998 and Human Rights Act 1998. However, the employer is likely to be at greater legal risk if it does not vet e-mails than it is from liability attaching to its breach of human rights in doing so. It is better to ban personal e-mails at work, tell employees that all their e-mails may be read, and then undertake checking than risk libellous or other unlawful e-mails being sent out.

Contracts and misrepresentation

Even more likely than libel is that the employee will send out an inaccurate or badly written e-mail, or one which is unauthorized but which may render the company liable for a contract formed thereby or a statement made in the e-mail. Liability in contract law or for misrepresentation or negligent misstatement under the law of tort may then arise.

The e-mail policy set out in Appendix 2 warns employees that their e-mails may be scrutinized by the employer.

Further information

A useful document, Data Protection Act 1998 *The Use of Personal Data Employer/Employee Relationships*, October 2000 Draft Code of Practice is on the UK Data Protection Registrar's Website at: <http://www.dataprotection.gov.uk>.

The Freedom of Information Act 2000 can be found at: <http://www.parliament.the-stationery-office.co.uk/pa/pabills.htm>.

The April 2000 Consultation Document *Competition in E-commerce* by Oftel and the Office of Fair Trading is on the Oftel Website at <http://www.oftel.gov.uk/superhwy/ecom0400.htm>.

The Electronic Commerce Directive 2000/31 was adopted on 8 June 2000, and published in OJ L178/1 on 17 July 2000.

The Regulation of Investigatory Powers Act 2000 and the Human Rights Act 1998 can be found at: <http://www.parliament.gov.uk>.

The Telecommunications Lawful Business Practice (Interception of Communications) Regulations (SI 2000/2699) can be found at: <http://www.hmso.gov.uk> by searching for 'Lawful Business Practice'.

2 TRADE MARKS, COPYRIGHT AND DATABASES: INTELLECTUAL PROPERTY

This chapter examines trade marks and copyright law as they apply to Websites and the use of ecommerce. It shows how to protect a domain name and what registration and dispute-resolution routes are possible.

The key issues for businesses are to ensure that the domain name they choose does not breach the trade mark rights of anyone else, nor that they copy any copyright works which belong to third parties, and that they acquire the rights which they need when they commission Website designs and material. They should also keep watch in case others infringe their rights, and act quickly if they do.

Trade marks

PICKING THE NAME

Companies will logically wish to pick their own business name as their Internet domain name. In the UK, the domain name may be a registered trade mark under the Trade Marks Act 1994. English case law, particularly *One in a Million*, has established that the registered trade mark will usually prevail over the registered domain name. So always consider the following courses of action:

- Conduct a trade mark search at the patent office (details of how to do so are at <http://www.patent.gov.uk>) before choosing or using a name, even if the domain name is available.
- Check at Companies House (<http://www.companieshouse.gov.uk>) as to whether anyone has registered that name as a limited company, which may show they have already built up 'goodwill' in that name, and means that even if they do not have a registered trade mark, they may have rights to stop use of the name through the law called 'passing off'.
- Ideally, carry out similar searches abroad too, as the domain name will be seen all over the world. In some cases, agreements with those with

similar names will need to be reached, with perhaps links to each other's sites.

● Check the usual trade mark steps, such as whether the name is in fact a rude word abroad, and register it in appropriate cases as a UK trade mark and/or community trade mark throughout the EU.

The Trade Marks Act 1994 protects registered trade marks. Registration is the best means of protecting a trade name. Registration of the name as a limited company at Companies House is not effective trade mark protection. Trade marks are registered for particular classes of goods or services. If a name is not registered, but goodwill and reputation have built up over the years in that name, English law may still protect it through the law of 'passing off'. However, this is harder to prove. The owner of the name has to show they have substantial reputation in the name, and that someone using it or using a similar logo, colour scheme or other features of a product is misrepresenting their business as that of the person who owns the name or other rights, and that damage has resulted. Confusion must also be shown.

Applying this to domain names on the Internet, someone running, for example, <cocacola.com> could be stopped because with such a well-known name the confusion could obviously be shown. However, with other less prominent names, it is not as easy to show the necessary confusion. Many of the trade mark disputes relating to domain names so far have arisen because of people having the same names. For example, the author practises as a solicitor under her own name, 'Singletons'. <Singletons.com> are hairdressing salons in the USA. They registered the name as a domain name first. They receive the rights.

In practice, businesses should seek advice from trade mark solicitors or trade mark agents such as those who are members of the Institute of Trade Mark Agents (<http://www.itma.org.uk>). New dot.coms should consider registration of their names as trade marks as well as domain names. The domain registration and subsequent trading may be enough to begin the process of accumulation of goodwill in the name and subsequent rights to sue for passing off, but it is much quicker and more effective to register a trade mark.

COMMUNITY TRADE MARKS

It is also possible to register one trade mark which applies throughout the whole of the EU – a Community Trade Mark (CTM). UK trade mark agents can also advise on these. They are cheaper than applying to register a national trade mark in each EU state. Registrations in other jurisdictions internationally are also a good idea where widespread use is envisaged, which of course it is with many Internet businesses.

WHEN TO REGISTER TRADE MARKS

In practice, registration is not always the most practical advice because it costs several hundred pounds to register a trade mark, and some new businesses cannot afford to do this. In such a case, a pragmatic approach should be taken. However, UK businesses should, wherever possible, register a trade mark in the UK or throughout the EU (the CTM) as a minimum. It also looks more professional on a Website to be able to say a trade mark is registered – the bigger companies register. Anyone hoping to build a valuable Web or other brand should register as soon as they can.

TRADE MARK SYMBOLS

The symbol for a registered trade mark is ®. It is an offence under the Trade Marks Act 1994 to claim that a mark is registered when it is not. It is also an offence to make unjustified threats of trade mark infringement, so be very careful about sending out warning letters or liability could arise. Have such letters checked by intellectual property lawyers first.

The symbol for an unregistered mark is ™. Some people think this means 'registered trade mark', but it does not.

Although it is not a legal obligation to display these symbols in order to claim the trade mark rights, it makes it harder for people infringing rights to claim they had no knowledge a mark was registered if the symbol is there. It warns people off.

SIMILAR NAMES

Trade mark registration is on the basis of classes of goods. Someone could register HAGGA for bread, and someone else HAGGA for nails. There would be no overlap and no confusion. This changes with the Internet, because use of a domain name is not in any particular class. Someone might do an Internet search for HAGGA, and they would find whichever of the two fictional companies had registered <www.hagga.com> first.

CASE EXAMPLES

British Telecommunications Plc **v.** *One in a Million Ltd* **[1998] FSR 265**

Facts BT, Marks & Spencer, Virgin and others were offered their own names as domain names by the defendant, who had registered them for the purpose of sale.

The Decision The Court of Appeal held that registration of someone's distinctive name as a domain name does amount to passing off, and is a breach of registered trade mark rights.

Comment This decision bolsters the position of the trade mark owner in fighting off those cashing in on a registration.

Prince **v.** *Prince* **(30 July 1997)**

Facts Prince plc was a UK IT services provider. Prince Sports Group Inc was a US sports company. The UK company registered <www.prince.com> as a domain name. It received a threatening letter from the US company, so the UK company sued for an unjustified threat of trade mark infringement.

The Decision It was held that it was an unjustified threat.

Comment This decision shows how important it is to ensure that threatening letters are properly checked by lawyers to ensure they do not in themselves amount to an offence.

World Wide Fund for Nature **v.** *World Wrestling Federation Entertainment Inc* **(Court of Appeal 27 February 2002,** *Times Law Report* **12 March 2002)**

Facts In this case the Court held that a settlement by which parties to a dispute resolved their differences should be respected. Both parties use the letters WWF and the world wild life fund reached an agreement with the wrestling company about use of the letters WWF some years ago. The wrestling body subsequently ignored the agreement, particularly from when it launched its Website in 2000 under <www.wwf.com> and they were successfully sued by the wildlife body in this result.

The Decision The court said that where the claimant had been a party to a settlement of a genuine dispute, designed to define the boundaries of his trading rights as against the defendant, he was entitled to expect that to be enforced. It was not for him to prove that it was reasonable. The presumption was that the restraints, having been agreed between the parties most involved, represented a reasonable division of their interests. It was for the defendant, seeking to avoid the agreement, to show that there was something which justified such a course, because the dispute was contrived, as in the *BAT* case; or because there was not reasonable basis for the rights claimed, as, apparently, in *Apple*; or because it was otherwise contrary to the public interest, for example, going beyond the legitimate purpose of seeking to avoid confusion or conflict between the parties.

Comment The case turned on a contract the two WWF bodies had signed but is also an interesting illustration of what happens when two parties in unrelated areas (wrestling and wildlife) go on line – both wanted wwf.com.

The case examples above illustrate the difference between the true 'cybersquatter' cashing in on a well-known name and trying to 'extract money with menaces' from the true owner, and the normal occurrence of two companies in different sectors having the same name.

In practice, if there are similar names, it is sensible for each party to arrange a hyperlink from their own Website to that of the confusingly similar company, so that neither loses business. If they are not in competition with each other, this is the most practical solution.

Another alternative is for one to buy the name of the other.

GENERIC NAMES

To avoid treading on the toes of another company, inventing a name is a good tactic. However, avoid names which are descriptive of a product or service. These have never been protected by trade mark law in most countries. For example, in 2000, 'efax' was held unprotectable for this reason when a legal dispute arose from two companies using the name on the Internet. The service was Internet faxing.

WRITING TO INFRINGERS

Where a business finds that its rights have been infringed, it will want to bring this to the attention of the infringing party, but being careful not to make an unjustified threat, which is against the law. Bear in mind the following points:

- Keep a watch for others using the same name, and take quick action, otherwise trade mark rights can be lost or jeopardized.
- Take legal advice before writing threatening letters, to avoid breaching trade mark law – unjustified threats are an offence.
- Send a letter before taking any legal action or pursuing a dispute-resolution procedure, because often a solution can be found quickly.

Here is the text of an example letter:

> It has recently come to our attention that you are using the name '____' as your domain name. Having taken legal advice, we believe this is an infringement of our registered UK [or Community] trade mark number 1234567 and/or amounts to passing off of our trade name/mark [____]. The purpose of this letter is

*to notify you of our rights and to require that
you give the undertakings attached to this letter
within [48] hours otherwise we shall have no
alternative but either to take legal action or
pursue the matter further through a dispute-
resolution body.*

The undertakings attached might ask for the use to cease, no further trade
mark infringements to occur, damages for any loss suffered to be paid, no
confusingly similar such use started in future, and legal costs to be paid.

US ANTI-CYBERSQUATTING CONSUMER PROTECTION ACT

This US law provides for civil liability for anyone who registers, traffics in
or uses a domain name that is confusingly similar or dilutes a trade mark
(provided the mark was distinctive/famous when the domain name was
registered) where the domain name is registered in bad faith or with an
intent to profit. Injunctions, orders for the name to be transferred and
damages or recovery of profits or statutory damages can be obtained. If
the company being sued cannot be tracked down, an order can still be
obtained.

People can claim their own name if someone else has registered it for profit.
In the UK, there have been some problems over those not trading in their
name, like certain footballers or authors, where they may have no 'goodwill'
in a trade mark sense. The police forces and Inland Revenue have tried to
wrest names from cybersquatters and come up against this issue.

The Act sets out factors used to assess whether a name has been registered
in bad faith or with an intent to profit:

1. Has the registrant any legitimate claim to trade mark rights in the name?
2. Are they using their own name in a bona fide way?
3. Are they making bona fide non-commercial use?
4. Are they trying to deceive customers for commercial gain or damage the
    goodwill of a third party?
5. Are they registering to make money, with no intention to make commer-
    cial use of the name?
6. Have they failed to provide correct contact details for the registry?
7. Have they 'warehoused' a large number of domain names which are
    third-party trade marks, whether they have offered to sell them or not?
8. Is the name very distinctive or famous?

DISPUTE-RESOLUTION: NAMES

In the UK, as seen above, a breach of trade mark may occur. This can lead to legal action in the courts. Court emergency injunctions can be obtained in a matter of days, or even hours in cases of extreme emergency. There is always a judge on duty, even at night. (The High Court of Justice, in London, can be telephoned on 020 7947 6000.) However, such protection can be very expensive. Typically, the parties would need to prepare a vast array of evidence for a judge. Witnesses swearing statements would be closeted with both their solicitor and specialist barrister for up to 12 hours a day. Many London firms would quote at least £50,000 legal fees to obtain an emergency interlocutory injunction. Many of those sued have no money – they are impoverished cybersquatters, so a high-profile decision may be a useful deterrent, but it is not usually a good source for costs recovery and damages.

Resolution of name disputes is increasingly referred not to court, but to alternative dispute-resolution methods. The two principal bodies used are the international naming body, ICANN, which will handle disputes for relatively modest cost (about £1000), and the World Intellectual Property Organization, based in Geneva, which also runs a cheap and quick resolution procedure. These bodies' decisions are not normally challenged in court afterwards, although in theory they could be. The result of an ICANN decision is that ICANN removes the name from the party concerned, who would have to go to court to retrieve it and for most cybersquatters that is not an economic option. These bodies can be contacted at <http://www.icann.org> and <http://www.wipo.org>. Both bodies follow the same Uniform Dispute Resolution Procedure (UDRP).

Copyright

Copyright protects literary, musical, artistic and similar works. It protects all written materials, sounds and drawings on Websites. The Copyright, Designs and Patents Act 1988 provides most of the protection. Copyright is not registered. It arises as soon as it is created, without formalities. It also protects computer software.

In practice, consider the following:

● Do not copy anything without permission.
● Do not assume that licences for one use cover other uses – they usually do not.

- Do not assume that a licence to one company in a group covers other companies in a group.
- Do not assume that a licence can be transferred to a third party.
- Do not assume that information in the public domain is free of copyright.
- In particular, watch out for databases. Buying a directory does not necessarily give the right to mail to customers in it. Fake addresses are lurking within to catch those breaching copyright and/or the new database right.
- *Always* make sure that everyone working on a product has a clear contract which states who owns the resulting rights.

Anyone engaging someone who is not an employee to work on their Website should make sure there is a written agreement in advance of the work being done, stating who will own any copyright and other intellectual property rights produced in the course of the work. If this is not done, the default position under the Copyright, Designs and Patents Act 1988 in the UK is that the *author*, not the person paying, owns the rights. The client buyer obviously receives a licence to use the work, but not exclusively, so other competitors could also be provided with that material.

This is one of the most popular misconceptions about copyright – that the person paying for the work will automatically own the copyright. It is actually the other way round, and many a copyright/Internet dispute has arisen over this issue. It is easily avoided by ensuring that before any work is done, the parties agree the position. They can reach agreement verbally (which is not ideal), or in a simple letter signed by both parties, or through a consultancy contract. Once the copyright work is created, the rights can be 'assigned' (transferred) later, but this is hard to achieve unless the designer wishes to arrange such an assignment. They may want additional fees if asked to assign later after the contract is made and the work done, or they may refuse altogether because they want to use the work on other Websites.

CHECKLIST: COPYRIGHT

- *Are we going to put existing copyright material on our Website?*
- *If yes, do we need permission from people such as the photographer who took the photographs for our paper corporate brochure and anyone else whose material will be put on the site?*
- *Who will arrange and pay for the permissions for the above material and any new material to be put on the Website?*

- *Do we have to put any copyright or trade mark notices on our Website?*
  Examples of such notices are given in the appendices, and may simply be
  '©ABC plc 2000' or may be a detailed notice about what can and cannot
  be done with copyright material on the site such as one might expect on
  a site with sample magazines or other free content.
- *Does the Web page designer want their name and details displayed on the site?*
  Did our contract with them deal with this? Have they asserted their 'moral
  rights' to be named as author?
  The Copyright, Designs and Patents Act 1988 allows the author of a
  copyright work to assert moral rights, including the right to be identified
  as the author of designs such as those appearing on a Website. A standard
  contract for a Web page design may exclude the moral rights.
- *Do we want to include a statement about hyperlinks to our sites on the*
  Website?
  Chapter 4 looks at links and the law. Some sites restrict linking except to
  the home page. Others have no restriction.

CONTRACTS AND INTELLECTUAL PROPERTY

Appendix 4 gives an example of a very simple contract with a sub-contrac-
tor/designer. However, anyone with a large Website design programme will
need to draw up a much more detailed agreement, probably using the
services of an Internet lawyer. Examples of contracts can be found at
<http://www.bitlaw.com/forms/index.html>, although most are US agree-
ments.

However, clause 5 of the agreement in Appendix 4 states that the rights in
the work will be owned by the buyer, which is the minimum protection
where bespoke work is commissioned. There will be cases where the customer does not mind if the designer will be using the same designs on other
Websites – indeed, the price is likely to be a lot cheaper if this is the case. It
is normally for the more expensive or very bespoke sites where the client/
user will want an exclusive licence of the copyright and other rights in the
site, or ownership of the rights.

If the designer is writing computer software to run on the site for the client,
the same issues arise. There are no moral rights, such as the right to be
identified as author, under the Copyright, Designs and Patents Act 1988,
but a contract term may still, if the designer chooses, require that their
name be put on all references to the software. The 'buyer' of software will
need access to the 'source code' of the software. The source code is the
secret coding of the software, which can be understood and copied by those
with the requisite knowledge and access to it. If the buyer will own all the

rights in the commissioned software, then it can require possession of the source code and all updates. If not, it can arrange for the source code to be deposited with a neutral third party, such as the NCC Group in Manchester, which runs a source code deposit 'escrow' service under which the source code is deposited. An escrow contract is then signed. This is standard in the IT industry.

Clause 6 in the contract in Appendix 4 requires the designer/sub-contractor to put all copyright notices required by the client on the works to be produced.

WARRANTIES AND INDEMNITIES

Whenever a copyright work is commissioned, it is sensible to extract a written promise from the supplier that they have not copied it from anyone else. If the designer does then breach that promise, an action for damages for breach of contract can be brought. That will not release the buyer from liability, however, even if the breach of copyright were innocent. It is therefore always best to use long-standing designers with good reputations. A designer giving a warranty may disappear when a legal action is brought, and the warranty may prove worthless.

Often, such a warranty is backed up with an 'indemnity' clause, as in clause 9 of the sample contract in Appendix 4. This is a promise to pay money – all money, or loss suffered by the buyer if such a breach of the warranty occurs. Although an indemnity is not essential, it is a useful addition, and means in practice that the supplier is likely to be legally obliged to pay more money sooner than is the case with a simple warranty, where an action for damages may have to be brought and the level of damages recoverable may be less.

In practice, some suppliers have a real fear of 'indemnities', and if contract negotiations reach a stalemate, a solution can be to drop the indemnity and keep the warranty. Whilst not offering as full protection as the indemnity, the buyer still has the benefit of a contractual promise that the work is not copied.

Other practical measures include the following:

- Look carefully at the work as it is produced. If there seem to be works on the site or designs which may be those of a third party, ask the designer whether this is the case and whether clearance has been obtained.
- Check that copyright notices are sufficiently prominent to deter illegal copying. Someone might be able to convince themselves, even if not a

court, that their copying was 'innocent' if they failed to spot a very small copyright notice on a home page. If such a notice is on every page of the site or particular documents on the site, that will act as a greater deterrent.

● Seek copyright consents. There is no need to assume that a copyright work cannot be used. Check whether a small licence fee may secure a right of use.

MUSIC

Anyone broadcasting music on their Website will need a licence to do so from the copyright owner. In most cases, in the UK a licence can be bought from the Performing Rights Society (<http://www.prs.co.uk>) or the MCPS (<http://www.mcps.co.uk>).

DRAWINGS AND PICTURES

Drawings and pictures on a Website will also be protected by copyright. Do not use a famous person's image without taking legal advice first.

POPULAR MYTHS: COPYRIGHT

Information in the public domain is free of copyright restrictions
Untrue. The information may not be confidential because it is published, but it is still protected by copyright.

If I pay for a copyright work, I will own it
Untrue. Unless otherwise agreed, all the buyer receives is a non-exclusive licence to use the work.

The advertising agency or Website designer will check the material for copyright purposes
Not necessarily. Not all agencies do this.

I can copy a certain percentage of a copyright work without breaching copyright
Untrue. There is no percentage. The courts look at whether a *substantial* part of the work is copied, and this may be a small but important part.

As long as I acknowledge the source, it is not breach of copyright
Untrue. Some people and some governments put up a notice on their Websites or other documents saying that they allow copying as long as the

source is acknowledged and the material is not altered. However, that would only apply to those who have released material on that basis.

I have been forwarded an e-mail, so the sender will have obtained copyright clearance
Untrue. Lots of people send documents attached to or within e-mails to which they do not own the rights, and then the recipient may breach the law.

Databases

A very important area to watch is that of databases. Many Websites provide access to databases, some on a chargeable basis. These may not always have copyright protection, but a new form of protection in the EU is called 'database right'. One of the most valuable assets of many companies is their customer list. Databases play an important role in businesses, and yet the legal issues surrounding them are not very well understood.

The databases generated by a company may be a valuable hidden asset. Simple measures, such as ensuring consents from individuals providing their data to particular future uses of the database, can enhance its value considerably. In law, many databases are protected by copyright. The English courts have for centuries protected mundane works in this way, from football pools coupons to lists of racing fixtures, whereas in some other EU states copyright has only been awarded to work of intellectual merit. It is not surprising, then, that whenever the European Commission seeks to harmonize any laws throughout the EU in this field, there is a conflict between EU states. This was resolved in relation to databases in 1996, when an EU directive harmonizing the law in this field was agreed.

However, before considering the law, businesses first need to know what databases there are in a company, to make sure they are properly looked after, to ensure they are protected, and to make sure databases are not used in breach of any existing licence contracts from the owners of those databases.

PRACTICAL QUESTIONS

Businesses should ask:

- *What databases do we have within the company, and in particular that will be used on or in connection with our Website? Does anyone keep a list? Who is responsible for them?*

- *Are they kept up to date?*
- *Do they involve 'personal data' under the Data Protection Act 1998?*
- *If so, are we properly registered under the Act?*
- *Do we have any problems with the 1998 Act in so far as data may be exported or not kept secure or up to date, or is it being used for purposes other than those for which it was obtained? If so, how can that be corrected?*
- *Have we checked that we comply with data protection law in relation to personal data put on Websites?*
  For example, photographs and personal details of staff on Websites should first be cleared with the individual concerned and also the copyright owner of the rights in the photograph.
- *Do we hold databases or personal data in manual form which now falls under the data protection legislation for the first time?*
- *Do our contracts, where they refer to the various 'intellectual property rights', refer not just to copyright, but also the new 'database right'?*
- *Do we deal with ownership of database and copyright in databases when we enter into contracts with third parties working on our data or gathering it for us, or do we make erroneous assumptions about who will own the rights?*
- *Do all members of staff know that they cannot simply conduct mass mailings from databases they come across, and that they may need consent from the owner of the rights in the database?*
  All relevant licences should be checked first.
- *Do we copy other people's databases, and therefore breach their rights?*
- *Do we check whether others are copying our databases, and take action where necessary? Do we include methods of catching out those who use our data, such as including false addresses to ensure that we pick up on infringements?*

DATABASE AND COPYRIGHT WARNING NOTICES FOR WEBSITES

In England, it is not necessary to put a warning notice on a copyright or database right-protected work before it obtains protection, but it is a sensible precaution as it warns infringers and makes it clear that the rights apply.

An example might be:

© E S Singleton 2000. All Rights Reserved.

or

Copyright and Database Rights

The material on this Website is protected by copyright and database right throughout the world, and [XYZ] is a registered trade mark. You may download and print from this site for personal and internal purposes but may not commercialize or otherwise copy the material in any way without our consent. Copyright queries should be addressed to Mrs E.S. Singleton, tel. (+44) (0)20 8866 1934, fax (+44) (0)20 8429 9212, e-mail <susan@singlelaw. com>, The Ridge, South View Road, Pinner, Middlesex HA5 3YD, UK.

or

COPYRIGHT and COPYING

Copying is only allowed in accordance with the following permissions:

1 You may view this page onscreen and print out a copy for personal use.
1 You may save a copy of this page to your local hard disk for the purposes of creating one personal backup copy.

All other copying and distribution of any of the contents of this site are strictly forbidden. This licence to copy does not permit incorporation of the material or any part of it in any other work or publication, whether in hard copy or electronic or any other form. In particular (but without limitation) no part of these Web pages may be distributed or copied for any commercial purpose. No part of these Web pages may be reproduced on or transmitted to or stored in any other Website or other form of electronic retrieval system nor may be accessed in such manner as to make them appear part of any third party's Website or electronic database or retrieval system.

WHICH DATABASES ATTRACT COPYRIGHT PROTECTION?

Under the UK Copyright and Rights in Databases Regulations 1997 (SI 1997/3032), original databases are protected by copyright. They are classed as 'original' where 'by reason of the selection or arrangement of the contents of the database the database constitutes the author's own intellectual creation'.

WHICH DATABASES ATTRACT DATABASE RIGHT PROTECTION?

Under the 1997 Regulations, a database will obtain the lesser database protection only for a period of 15 years where there has been 'substantial investment in obtaining, verifying or presenting the contents of the database'. Many databases involve little intellectual creation – for example, an alphabetical listing would not – but they do involve a lot of investment in putting the data together. The 1997 Regulations make it clear there would be protection even if there is no intellectual creativity, as long as there has been such investment. If an individual has used computer software they have licensed to do all the work, it is possible they will not have put in any substantial investment.

The database itself, whether protected by copyright or database right or both, is defined as a 'collection of independent works, data or other materials are arranged in a systematic or methodical way and are individually accessible by electronic or other means'.

EXAMPLE: OWNERSHIP OF RIGHTS

A large company commissions a market research body to undertake market studies for it and to gather data. The contract does not contain any clauses about database or copyright right. At the end of the year, the company serves notice to terminate the agreement. Who owns the rights? Where the database is protected by copyright, in most cases the rights actually remain with the author. The research body is not an employee of the large company, so there is no automatic vesting of copyright in the company paying for the work to be done. Instead, all the buyer receives is a licence to use the rights. The author encountered a real dispute along these lines. The client research company was able to extract over £20,000 in additional fees on termination in order to transfer the rights to the buyer, which, had the buyer's legal department dealt with it in the original agreement, would not have had to be paid. This is therefore an important issue which should not be overlooked.

DATABASE RIGHT

Some databases are so mundane that they receive just 'database right'. In these cases, the ownership position is slightly less clear, as the legislation refers to the 'maker' of the database owning the rights, in default of agreement. This is the person who takes the initiative in obtaining, verifying or presenting the contents of a database, and assumes the risk of investing in this. 'Assuming the risk' suggests that the person paying is the maker, as does the 'taking of the initiative'. It is ludicrous that the ownership on database right and copyright should differ. There is already a difference between the position on ownership of copyright and ownership of design right (a right protecting the appearance of articles), where, under designs law, the person commissioning the design will own the rights if there is no agreement stating otherwise. Databases receive database right rather than copyright where they are not a work of intellectual creativity. It is always important to check when the database was created, however, because before 1 January 1998 the only protection was by copyright, and transitional arrangements may apply to older databases. This is the sort of area where, if there is a problem, legal advice should be sought.

POPULAR MYTHS: DATABASES

Finally, let us unmask some common myths about databases:

We bought the directory, therefore we can mail or e-mail the people in it

Untrue. In fact most directories, contain false or 'seed' addresses of directors or employees to catch out people exploiting the directory in this way. It may be possible to negotiate a licence to mail people in the directory, but payment will normally be required.

We paid for the directory to be put together, so it is our intellectual property

Untrue in most cases, unless there is agreement to the contrary. Make sure contracts with third parties say that all rights will be owned by the company paying for the work. Under the Copyright, Designs and Patents Act 1988 for databases protected by copyright, the default position is that the company doing the work keeps the copyright, and the client simply obtains a licence to use. This may be sufficient, but it does not stop the database compiler using the databases for other clients, unless there is agreement prohibiting this, of course.

We have received a licence to use a database, so we can use it throughout the world

The licence may only give rights of use in the UK. Read the terms carefully. Also, if the database contains 'personal data' under the Data Protection Act 1998, which came into force on 1 March 1998, then export out of the European Economic Area to countries without adequate data protection laws may be prohibited. In 2000, the EU and USA reached agreement on export of data to the USA – a 'Safe Harbor Agreement' – and the Information Commissioner has issued recent Advice on export of data (see 'Further information' below).

The database is just names and addresses, so it will not be protected by copyright

It is true that from 1 January 1998, when the new database right came into force, new databases which are not works of intellectual creativity (for example, mere alphabetical listings) do not receive copyright protection. However, most which have resulted from substantial investment are protected by database right.

We have rekeyed all the data and could have found it out from other sources, so we cannot have breached anyone's right

Whether it has been rekeyed, scanned or copied electronically or by copier does not matter. It is still copying, and whether the information is available in the public domain does not stop it being protected by copyright. A licence is required. Making a few changes will have no impact either.

Patents

Trade marks and copyright and database right are the main intellectual property rights likely to be relevant to most Internet businesses. However, sometimes there is a novel idea which is protectable by a registered patent under the Patents Act 1977 or equivalent foreign legislation. Here, it is definitely essential to take advice from patent agents, such as those who are members of the Chartered Institute of Patent Agents (<www.cipa.org.uk>).

Most new 'ideas' for Internet businesses are not patentable. They are not 'industrial inventions'. They can be protected in the initial stages by tight confidentiality agreements, but once they are in use they are no longer secret and anyone can copy them. Of course, the words on the Website and name of the business cannot be copied, but the way it is organized can. There are some areas where patents have been obtained. Patent litigation is currently being conducted, for example, by a company which claims to have registered as a patent the technology which allows customers placing a second order on a Website to avoid the need to re-send their card and other details, so their future orders are processed more quickly. Anyone licensing technology protected by patent should obtain a warranty and indemnity from the licensor that there is no patent dispute going on and that the licensor will pay the licensee any costs and damages which arise from breach of rights.

Registered designs

The final intellectual property right is design right, which protects the appearance of articles. For example, many of the clothes or articles of furniture sold on Websites have registered design protection. The design of certain three-dimensional articles may be protected by unregistered design right, but this is unlikely to be relevant to ecommerce.

The Registered Designs Regulations 2001 implemented the EU designs directive in the UK in December 2001. Designs law now protects computer typefaces and fonts. The Community Design Regulation came into force in March 2002 and provides for a new unregistered EU design right and institutes an EU-wide registered 'Community Design Right' available from 2003.

Further information

The UK Performing Rights Society Website is: <http://www.prs.co.uk>.

The UK Patent Office Website at <http://www.patent.gov.uk> contains useful information on intellectual property law, and information on database law can be found at various locations on that site by searching for 'database'.

For a very comprehensive listing of all contact details of many copyright and related organizations in the UK, see the 'Useful contacts' part of the Website of MCPS (the Mechanical Copyright Protection Society) at: <http://www.mcps.co.uk>.

Examples of contracts relating to Internet law can be found at: <http://www.bitlaw.com>.

The EU database directive is Directive 96/9/EC of the European Parliament and of the Council of 11 March 1996 on the legal protection of databases, OJ L 077, 27 March 96 p.20. The text can be found at: <http://www.europa.eu.int/eur-lex/en/lif/dat/1996/en_396L0009.html>.

The UK Copyright and Rights in Databases Regulations 1997 (SI 1997/3032) which implement the directive are on the HMSO Website at: <http://www.legislation.hmso.gov.uk/si/si1997/1973032.htm>.

A useful book on database law is *Database Law* by Christopher Rees and Simon Chalton of law firm Bird and Bird, published by Jordans in 1998.

For issues relating to the Data Protection Act 1998 and personal data, see the Website at <http://www.dataprotection.gov.uk> and Tolley's *Data Protection: Handbook*, a textbook on the 1998 Act by Susan Singleton (2002).

Legal advice on database right and other intellectual property issues can be obtained from solicitors who specialize in this field, details of which appear in the Chambers & Partners' legal directory which is available at: <http://www.chambersandpartners.com>.

3 JURISDICTION AND ADVERTISING ON THE WEB

This chapter considers some of the major legal areas arising from those uses of the Internet to which laws apply, and jurisdiction to advertising law in general. It also covers data protection (including export of personal data). Appendix 3 gives an example of some standard terms and conditions for use on a Website.

Advertising law is a vast topic, and this chapter does no more than mention some of the principal issues arising. Data protection law is covered in particular, as vast amounts of individuals' 'personal data' is handled over the Internet, and since 1 March 2000 much stricter rules have applied in the UK.

Jurisdiction and disputes

Where should a case go to court if a British and a foreign supplier are involved? Normally, the contract will stipulate, but if not, then the law must decide the matter. The European Commission has issued a very important new regulation (*The regulation on jurisdiction and the recognition and enforcement of judgments in civil and commercial matters*, Reg 44/2001 (OJ 16 January 2001 L121). It determines where legal disputes will be heard, whether in the country of the seller or the buyer, will have special rules to protect consumers, and might well, in the final text, provide that consumers have a right to be sued in their home state, not the seller's country. The most controversial issue in it is whether a Website can specify local, for example English law, and then be sure only English law will apply, or whether a consumer in, say, Germany would be entitled to invoke German law and jurisdiction. The UK Department of Trade and Industry (DTI) had proposed a compromise that if the Website is 'directed' at a particular foreign territory, then the consumer can bring proceedings in their home state, but if the Website is just a general site not directed at the consumer's territory, then the supplier could be confident that only its own local law would apply. On 7 April 2000, the DTI published its consultation paper on this. On 22 December the regulation 44/2001 was adopted.

Most countries, including those of the EU but not the US, have agreed to the Rome Convention and the Brussels Convention. These are made part of English law in the UK by the Contract Applicable Law Act 1990 and the Civil Jurisdiction and Enforcement of Judgments Act 1982. The essence of these is that if a particular law and jurisdiction is chosen by the parties to an agreement, then that will prevail. If they have not made a choice, then these rules state what happens. In many cases, the laws with the closest connection to the contract will then apply. The regulation makes a major distinction between contracts with consumers, and other contracts. Both are examined below.

Anyone domiciled in an EU member state should be sued in that home state. The regulation does not apply to bankruptcy or winding up proceedings, cases about the legal status of people or companies, matrimonial proceedings or cases relating to wills and succession, social security and arbitration. Article 60 of the regulation stipulates what 'domicile' means. For companies, this means the place which is their 'statutory seat, central administration or principal place of business'. So a company which is registered at Companies House as an English company is domiciled there, even if it does some business in, say, France.

In April 2000, the UK Inland Revenue, pre-empting OECD discussions, said businesses should not be able to claim tax residence in the UK (and thus benefit from its relatively liberal tax regime) simply through location of a server there.

Article 3 of the regulation provides that only in limited cases can someone be sued in a different country from where they are domiciled. However, these limited cases are important. In cases relating to performance of a contract, which is the most relevant area in business, then someone can be sued in the courts in a different member state from their domicile for the place of performance of the contractual obligation (Article 5(1)(a)). The parties can agree where the place of performance is.

Therefore, the simple, practical answer in order to obtain legal certainty (with the exception of consumer contracts – see below) is to have a clause in all contracts saying that the contract will be performed in a particular place.

Many sellers will want their own laws and courts to handle disputes, but if they obtain a judgment against a defendant, they will still have to go to that defendant's country to enforce the judgment (get the money), so they may want to retain an option to sue in the home country in any event. Legal advice should be sought on these issues, as they are complicated. In law, there is no reason why the provisions have to be fair and balanced.

The supplier can give itself the option of suing in its own or the buyer's jurisdiction, whilst restricting the buyer to suing in the seller's country. This point alone illustrates well the advantages of a business using its own standard conditions of sale, which will include points such as this which favour that party.

If the parties have not agreed otherwise, then the place of performance is the place where goods are delivered under the contract or should have been delivered, or for services, the place where the services are provided (Article 5(1)(b)).

EXAMPLE

Company A in the UK sells a large industrial machine to B, a French company. The sale is on A's standard terms of sale. They state that the English courts have exclusive jurisdiction relating to all disputes, and that the place of performance of the contract is the UK. The French company can be sued in the UK.

If instead there were no contract and the parties had not agreed a place of performance and A delivers the goods to B in France, then B must be sued in France.

If, again with no contract or agreement on the issue, B collects the goods in the UK, using its own carrier, ex works from A, then the place of delivery is the UK, and presumably English (or Scots law, as the case may be) will apply.

If services are provided and there is no agreement about a contract and place of supply, then the courts where the services are provided have jurisdiction. This is easy enough to check for many services contracts, such as those requiring attendance at premises for remedial maintenance, but not so clear where services are provided remotely offsite, through a telephone hotline, fault-solving by e-mail, downloaded fixes, and so on.

SPECIAL RULES

There are special rules for many other types of arrangements which are not considered here, such as criminal matters, disputes with branches or agencies, cargo salvage, and so on. If a person is one of a number of defendants, then they may be able to be sued elsewhere if it is expedient that their case be heard with those of other defendants. Section 3 (Articles 8–14) of the regulation deals entirely with contracts for insurance.

CONSUMER CONTRACTS

Article 16 of the regulation provides that a consumer can bring proceedings against the other party to a contract either in the consumer's home country or the other party's home country, whereas the consumer can only be sued in their own country. It is particularly important to take legal advice if a consumer contract is involved, as there are many laws around the world which protect consumers. In practice, most ebusiness is conducted between two businesses, not the business-to-consumer transactions which appear to receive most of the publicity.

Example: Consumers

Consumer B buys a computer game from a Website in the UK. B lives and works in Greece. The game does not work. B can choose whether to sue in the UK or Greece. If instead B does not pay, the UK supplier must sue B in Greece.

There are exceptions allowing the parties to agree, after a dispute has arisen, to submit to the jurisdiction of certain courts and to keep the consumer to the country where they were domiciled if the supplier is domiciled there (if the consumer moves later, if the contract provides for this they can be forced to stick with the country from which they first came). This last point will need to be reflected in contracts in due course if suppliers want to benefit from this.

EMPLOYMENT CONTRACTS

The provisions in Section 5 (Articles 18–23) of the regulation are similar to those relating to consumer contracts. The employee can only be sued in their home country. The employer can be sued in its own country or that of the employee, at the employee's option.

CHOICE

Article 23 of the regulation says that if the parties agree in writing, including any communication by electronic means which provides a durable record of the agreement, particular courts will then have jurisdiction that will prevail. This is interesting because it appears to cover the same ground as Article 5(1)(b), which lets the parties agree the place of performance (and thus the jurisdiction) in cases relating to contract and does not appear to be without prejudice to the consumer provisions (in other words, under Article 23 it appears that even consumers can have a foreign jurisdiction forced upon them by a contract term). This may not be what was intended, however.

RECOGNITION OF FOREIGN JUDGMENTS

Chapter III of the regulation deals with recognition of foreign judgments by courts in other EU states. No special procedures must be necessary for the recognition of a foreign judgment. This means that if an English company obtains a court judgment in England, then it should be able to take it to a court in another EU state, and the court should allow enforcement (such as seizure of property or sending in bailiffs, or otherwise ensuring payment is received) without any difficult or special hurdles being put in its way.

DTI CONSULTATION DETAILS

The DTI examined the Brussels Convention, in particular Article 13, which confers jurisdiction over disputes between a consumer and a business in the courts of the consumer's country of domicile. It allows consumers to bring actions in their own states. As the DTI says:

> Websites are generally accessible from anywhere. Therefore a trader with a website might be said to be directing its activities to all EU countries.

If this is the case, then consumers would be given rights to sue at home whether or not they had been deliberately targeted there. The DTI says that online businesses could not limit their exposure by stipulating which member state they were targeting, and a business targeting only its national market would be deemed to be targeting other states and may find itself in litigation abroad in countries it was not targeting. It is possible that the final version of the proposed regulation will allow consumers to contract out of this provision, and thus choose to be sued in the seller's state. However, there is much resistance to this because, in practice, consumers will have no power to negotiate against such a contractual requirement in any event.

KEY POINTS: JURISDICTION

- State on the Website any countries from which orders are not accepted (for example, countries where it is illegal to sell the goods).
- State in the terms and conditions of sale on the Website which country's laws apply to the contract and where disputes will be heard. Also state where the 'place of performance of the contract is' (these words are used in the EU regulation).
- Be aware that some states will apply their local laws no matter what is provided in any contract.
- Take legal advice in particular where sales to consumers are involved, as in some cases the choice of law clause may not work.
- Do not be put off by the jurisdiction complications of the Internet. Whilst there are examples of foreign courts applying their laws to UK traders on the Internet, most business proceeds smoothly with no obscure foreign laws causing any problems.
- Consider whether business justifies having a foreign-language, local law Website with terms vetted under the local law.

Advertising law

There are many pieces of legislation relating to advertising law. They cannot all be covered here, so advice should be sought. Anyone wanting, for example, to use a competitor's trade mark to compare products or prices on a chart on a Website should take account of the Control of Misleading Advertisements Regulations 1988 (SI 1988/915) as amended by the Control of Misleading Advertisements (Amendment) Regulations 2000 (SI 2000/914) with effect from 23 April 2000, when the EU Comparative Advertising Directive 97/55 (OJ L290/18, 23 October 97) was implemented in the UK.

A useful Website on US advertising law can be found at: <http://www.arentfox.com/quickGuide/businessLines/advert/advertisingLaw/advertisinglaw.html>.

BRITISH CODES OF ADVERTISING AND SALES PROMOTION

All advertisements in the UK must be legal, decent, honest and truthful, in order to comply with the Codes of Advertising Practice (<http://www.asa.org.uk>). The Codes apply to advertisements in electronic material and in non-broadcast electronic media. They do not apply to broadcast commercials, which are the responsibility of the Independent Television Commission or the Radio Authority. The codes list about 200 statutes which apply, from the Betting and Gaming Duties Act 1981 to the Knives Act 1997, the Defamation Act 1996 to the Competition Act 1998, and the Trading Schemes Act 1996 to the Surrogacy Arrangements Act 1985. Legal advice should be sought. Do not rely on an Internet design company or even an advertising agency to advise or be liable for any breaches of the law contained in an advertisement. Check the advertisement closely, even when it has been written by an advertising agency.

A useful Website on marketing law is published online by solicitors Osborne Clark at: <http://www.marketinglaw.co.uk>.

Gathering personal data on Websites

Most businesses know that they need to notify ('register', as it used to be called) under the Data Protection Act 1998, which came into force on 1 March 2000. These laws apply throughout the EU, and in many other countries too. They are designed to protect personal information about individuals.

All UK businesses, whether involved with the Internet or not, are likely to handle personal data, and most will need to notify.

Personal data includes information such as lists of names and addresses. Of course, it also includes the information individuals send to companies when registering for product guarantees or completing 'surveys', and when online registration forms are completed on Websites.

CHECK FOR REGISTRATION UNDER THE DATA PROTECTION ACT

It is the data protection implications relating to Websites which are considered here. The first item to check is that your business has actually registered under the Act in the first place. Parent companies cannot register on behalf of all their subsidiaries. Each legal entity has to register. It is easy to check, because everyone registered is listed on <http://www.dpr.gov.uk>.

CHECK WHETHER THE BUSINESS HAS A PRIVACY POLICY ON ITS WEBSITE

Secondly, look at your corporate Website. Does it contain any information about data protection on it? If not, consider adding it. The best Websites have 'privacy policies' which tell users how their personal data will be used. There are examples on the Website of the UK Information Commissioner at <http://www.dataprotection.gov.uk>, and a full, thorough US version can be found at <http://www.dell.com>.

THE PADLOCK SYMBOL

In April 2000 the UK Information Commissioner, issued a new symbol:

The padlock symbol is to be used on forms when personal data is obtained from individuals, so they know that their personal details are being gathered. It can be used on Websites and other places. It is described as a 'signpost' by the Commissioner in a new leaflet on her Website at <http://www.dataprotection.gov.uk>. The leaflet is a very useful summary of obligations under the Act. The symbol can be downloaded as a graphics file from that Website, specifically to encourage its use on Websites, leaflets and other materials used to gather personal data.

INTERNET GUIDELINES FOR DATA CONTROLLERS

The following guidelines for consumers have been issued by the Commissioner:

> ### Data Controllers – Protection of Privacy on the Internet
>
> *In using the Internet for their business dealings, data controllers must take into account the privacy rights of individuals and their own responsibilities under privacy and data protection legislation. The following points should be considered by data controllers in planning their Internet strategies.*
>
> - *Personal data placed on the Internet is available world-wide. In many countries the*

use of personal data is not protected by
legislation. Because of this it is always
advisable and will often be essential to obtain
consent from individuals before publishing
their personal data on your website.

- When collecting information via the Internet
**always inform the user of who you
are**, what personal data you are collecting,
processing and storing and for what purpose.
Do this before a user gives you any information, when they visit your site and wherever
they are asked to provide information, for
example via an on-line application form. It
is good practice to ask for consent for the
collection of all data and it is usually
essential to get consent if you want to process
sensitive personal data.

- It is good practice for a data controller who
sets up a website to provide a statement of its
privacy policy. A 'privacy statement' helps
individuals to decide whether or not to visit
a site and, when they do visit, whether or not
to provide any personal information to the
data controller.

- Always let individuals know when you
intend to use 'Cookies' or other covert
software to collect information about them.

- **Never collect or retain personal data
unless it is strictly necessary for
your purposes.** For example you should
not require a person's name and full address
to provide an on-line quotation. If extra
information is required for marketing
purposes this should be made clear and the
provision of the information should be
optional.

- Design your systems in such a way as to
avoid or minimise the use of personal data.

- Upon a user's request you should **correct,
change or delete inaccurate details.** If
information is altered notify the third parties
to whom the original information was
communicated. **Regularly delete data**

which is out of date or no longer required.

- *Stop processing data if the user objects to it because the processing is causing them damage or distress.*
- *Only use personal data collected on-line for marketing purposes where the user has already been told that his or her information was to be used in this way. If a user asks you to stop using his or her data for marketing purposes you must do so and the individual should always be given the opportunity to opt out of the use of his or her data for marketing. It is also good practice to get the individual's consent before using their information for marketing. It will always be necessary to get their consent where the data is sensitive.*
- *Use the most up to date technologies to protect the personal data collected or stored on your site. Especially sensitive or valuable information, such as financial details should be protected by reliable encryption technologies.*

January 2000 Version 4, reproduced with permission of the Information Commissioner.

These rules above are a useful summary for those operating Websites. The UK legislation applies when the data controller is established in the UK or is processing data in the UK. It does not matter whether the data is that of UK citizens or not. The Information Commissioner has also issued compliance advice on 'Subject access to personal data contained in e-mails' (14 June 2000: <http://www.ccta.gov.uk/dpr/dpdoc.nst>).

In 2001 the Information Commissioner issued some detailed Frequently Asked Questions as regards the Internet and data protection which are available on the Website <www.dataprotection.gov.uk>.

ENSURING COMPLIANCE

Most of those involved with business networks will be most concerned as to what information must be placed on the Website. If no personal data is gathered, then no notice needs to be placed. However, check whether photographs, personal profiles or other personal data are included in the site content itself. Consent from employees for their details to be displayed in this way and probably 'exported' should be obtained in order to comply with the Act. Export of data from the European Economic Area (EEA) is a breach of the 8th Data Protection Principle in some cases if consent is not obtained. This is dealt with below.

EXPORT OF DATA AND THE DATA PROTECTION ACT 1998

The 1998 Act's general aim is to ensure that personal data is properly protected. It is a privacy measure. It is principally directed at ensuring that details about 'living individuals' are protected. The Act's general provisions are well described elsewhere, not least on the Website of the UK Information Commissioner (see 'Further information' below). Those holding personal data must register with the Commissioner, and must follow the provisions of the Act, including complying with eight data protection 'principles' and other obligations, such as the right of individuals to be given copies of the personal data held about them. Individuals are also given a right to object to direct marketing. Incorrect data must be rectified, and there are stringent new enforcement powers which can be used against companies which do not comply. In addition, in certain cases, individuals can be personally fined under the Act.

Examples of personal data include names and addresses of individual customers (including sole traders and partnerships), many e-mail addresses, photographs of individuals, and moving pictures of them. Anyone faxing a CV abroad or taking their PC abroad on a business trip outside the EEA ought to check how they can ensure compliance with the 8th Principle. Those businesses which e-mail personal data for processing to countries where labour costs are cheaper should also take advice. Companies with subsidiaries outside the EEA should take legal advice on the 8th Principle.

JURISDICTIONAL AMBIT

It is important, given the international nature of the Internet, to know in what countries it applies:

- The Act applies where the data controller is established in the UK, or for foreign businesses, where the processing of their data is carried on in the UK.
- The Act applies to data about individuals. It does not matter whether the data is 'foreign data'. For example, a list of customers in Australia would be 'data' under the Act, and the legislation would apply if it were processed in the UK or by a data controller based in the UK.
- The Act applies throughout the UK, but not on the Isle of Man, Guernsey or Jersey.
- The provisions restricting export of data from the EEA mean export from Austria, Belgium, Denmark, Finland, France, Germany, Greece, Iceland, Ireland, Italy, Liechtenstein, Luxemburg, The Netherlands, Norway, Portugal, Spain, Sweden and the UK. (These are the EEA countries, and data can be freely exported between these countries.)
- These provisions apply to 'transfer' of data, not to 'transit'. 'Transit' is defined by the Commissioner as meaning where data simply passes through another country. A transfer may occur where there are 'substantial processing' operations en route.
- The Act applies if the data is 'personal data' as defined in the Act in the UK, but also if it avoids being personal data for some reason (for example, it is manual data and is not part of a 'relevant filing system', and so falls outside the Act), but when transferred, for example by fax or telephone, to a colleague abroad will then be entered on a computer or kept in a relevant filing system. The Act would still then apply.

THE 8TH PRINCIPLE

The 8th Data Protection Principle provides that: 'personal data shall not be transferred to a country or territory outside the EEA unless that country or territory ensures an adequate level of protection for the rights and freedoms of data subjects in relation to the processing of personal data'.

APPROVED LIST

In September 2000, the European Commission was considering the data protection laws of a number of non-EU countries, to ascertain whether those states provide adequate protection for personal data transferred from the EU. Countries that are considered to do so will be subject to a 'Community Finding', allowing EU data controllers to transfer personal data to those states without further consideration of the adequacy of the protection provided for the data transferred. UK data controllers will be able to transfer personal data to any country subject to a 'Community Finding', and comply with the 8th Principle on that basis.

SWITZERLAND AND HUNGARY

The Commission has adopted a 'Decision' to the effect that Switzerland and Hungary provide adequate protection for personal data transferred to those countries from the EU. Over time, a number of other countries will appear on the Commission 'approved list'. The Commission has stated that it will shortly start the process of determining whether Canada's new privacy law provides adequate protection.

The Commission decisions can be found at: <http://europa.eu.int/eur-lex/en/oj/2000/1_21520000825en.html>.

THE USA: THE 'SAFE HARBOR AGREEMENT'

On 27 July 2000, the European Commission adopted a 'Decision' approving the US 'safe harbor' arrangement. This involves organizations in the USA committing themselves to comply with a set of data protection principles backed up by guidance provided through a number of 'frequently asked questions'. Commitment to 'safe harbors' will provide an adequate level of protection for transfers of personal data to the USA from EU member states. The Information Commissioner says: 'This will of course provide a basis for compliance with the 8th Principle of the DP Act in the UK in relation to transfers to US organisations that have signed up to the scheme. At the date of writing only 12 companies had signed up to the scheme in a very disappointing start. It is the view of the Information Commissioner that it is now time to see how the scheme works in practice. If problems do arise, then appropriate remedial action can be taken.

For further detailed information, see: <http://europa.eu.int/comm/internal_market/en/media/dataprot/news/safeharbor.htm>.

CONSENT

All these problems can be avoided if the individual has given their consent to the export of the data. In many cases this is possible, and then no consideration would need to be given to 'adequacy' and whether the country was on an approved list. Appendix 1 of the Act sets out the principles, and paragraph 13 describes what amounts to an 'adequate level of protection' before an export can take place. It also says that if processing falls within Schedule 4, then the 8th Principle will not apply.

Schedule 4 says that the 8th Principle will not apply where the individual ('data subject') has given consent to the transfer or where the transfer is necessary to perform a contract, and some other cases, such as public interest, legal proceedings, a transfer on terms approved by the UK Commissioner (the Confederation of British Industry (CBI) has issued some proposed model terms which will be e-mailed to callers free on request – tel. 020 7395 8247).

In July 2001 Model Standard Contractual Clauses for data export were agreed by the European Commission for export of personal data from the EU to data controllers and in 2002 similar clauses for export to data processors. By having the recipient abroad sign these clauses the EU sender of the data can be sure the 8th principle is followed.

One of the hardest questions under the 1998 Act in general is what is meant by 'consent'. It is particularly important because under the 'fair processing code' imposed by the 1st Principle of the Act, data should only be processed if the individual has 'given consent', and for 'sensitive personal data' such as data about sex, race or political opinions, the consent must be explicit. The Commissioner's view is that consent in many cases must be given by an active step by the individual. In other words, requiring customers to indicate if they 'do not' want their data passed on is normally not good enough any more. This has a major implication for the way forms and notices in paper and electronic form are handled. Individuals should now 'opt in' to their data being used in other ways, rather than 'opting out' as was often previously the case.

The 8th Principle does not apply if the individual gives consent. In her 'Advice' on this topic, the Commissioner gives examples of what consent may be allowed and what may not. For example, simply requiring individuals to sign to agree to any transfer of their data abroad where business needs require it is not enough, whereas a consent to pass details of a mortgage application to ABC Ltd in Singapore, which processes the mortgage on their behalf, and telling the customer that Singapore does not have a data protection law would be a proper consent (assuming the customer did indeed give the consent by signing or indicating consent electronically). Passing personnel records to a subsidiary abroad would also require a consent, as would passing information about the data subject and their insurance to companies outside the EEA where 'reinsurance' takes place.

There is also a right, even where there is no consent, to export data where it is 'necessary' to perform a contract. The Commissioner takes a narrow view of this. For example, it is said that if a UK retailer decides to locate its accounts department abroad, it is not necessary for the data to be shipped abroad to be processed. The data controller has 'chosen' to structure its business this way. It did not have to do so. In such a case, consent should be obtained if adequacy requirements cannot be met.

There are many other interesting issues relevant to the export of data which the 'Further information' given below addresses. Many companies are now seeking legal advice on their obligations in relation to export of data, or are asking the Information Commissioner for her views.

Terms and conditions on Websites

The appendices give some examples of a privacy policy and other notices for Websites, including terms for use of a bulletin board. Many sites will need more detailed terms too. The set in Appendix 3 cover use of a site, and also use of the services on the site which put the users in contact with suppliers of particular services without the site operators contracting directly for provision of those services. Chapter 5 examines the issues surrounding entering into contracts on the Internet.

CASE EXAMPLE

Japan

The Facts   On 30 March 2000, the Osaka District Court held that a hyperlink breached local law. A Japanese man marketed his image-processing software *FL Mask*, on his Website. It allowed those using the software to remove the photomask often used in Japan to censor explicit parts of photographic images. On the Website, he gave links to pornographic sites so that people could use his software to view those sites without restriction. The issue was whether the mere linking was an offence.

The Decision   The court found that in Japan, in this case there had been a breach of the law. The defendant received a one-year prison sentence suspended for a year. The judge decided that the offender had increased the number of ways to access obscene sites, and had made it easier for many people to view porno-graphic pictures, and that he was therefore guilty of aggra-vating crime.

Comment   If similar rules applied in the UK, for example, and were applied to other breaches of the law, someone wanting to display material which the English courts had banned, provocatively saying 'We cannot show you this as the English courts have banned it, but you can find it on a US server at ——', might breach the law. However, this is unlikely. It would be akin to telling people where they can go when on holiday in New York to pick up copies of a novel banned in the UK.

HYPERLINKS

One of the most useful aspects of the Internet is the ability to jump from one site to another using a hypertext link. Most companies are delighted to be linked with others. Usually, it means more publicity.

Indeed, one of the best things a new company can do to increase sales via the Internet is to ensure that its IT advisers have it listed and linked in as many ways as possible.

Linking and fees

Linking of Websites is not normally regarded as a breach of rights. In the US some companies however make a term, a contractual term, for use of their site, that linking requires a fee and this approach would probably be enforceable in the UK under the law of contract. The *Albuquerque Journal* Charges $50 for the right to link to each of its articles. <Localbusiness.com> and <Latino.com> are more generous, and permit one to five links without payment.

Haymarket and Burma Castrol

On 9 January 2001 Haymarket, the publisher, began legal action against Burmah Castrol, the oil company, in the UK for infringement of intellectual property rights. According to the *Financial Times* (10 January 2001) the complaint is about links on Castrol's web site <http://complete-motoring.com>, which 'frame' content from two of Haymarket's sites, <whatcar.com> and <autosport.com> within a Castrol-branded border, without permission and without payment of royalties. Breach of copyright and passing off are claimed.

The Castrol site makes reference to links on its home page and says:

> This Website contains links to Websites operated by parties other than Castrol. Such links are provided for your convenience only. Castrol does not control such Websites, and is not responsible for their contents nor shall Castrol be liable for any loss suffered as a result of the use thereof. Castrol's inclusion of links to such Websites does not imply any endorsement of the material on such Websites or any association with their operators.

Clicking on the Magazines section of the Castrol site (10 January 2001) brings up '*What Car?*' magazine which is reproduced on the site below the Castrol banner headline with the magazine appearing below it.

StepStone and Ofir

An online recruiter called StepStone became, it was claimed, the first company to use the EU database directive to stop a company linking its site to another. The company obtained an injunction against a Danish company, Ofir, to stop the link. StepStone said Ofir was using StepStone advertisements to make it appear more jobs were on offer through the Ofir site and the linking to the StepStone site meant people missed the StepStone home page. Adrian Lifely, at solicitors Osborne Clarke, for StepStone, said the linking had breached StepStone's intellectual property rights because of the provisions of the database directive. 'I am not aware of any other cases tried under the new EU regulations,' he was reported as saying. 'It is not, of course, every case of hypertext linking which is unlawful – the internet would grind to a halt. But the courts in Europe do have power to intervene where linking is extensive and prejudicial to the site involved.' A substantial part of the StepStone data was used without consent. The German court held that Ofir used the StepStone job advertising as its own and there was a risk Ofir would take business away from StepStone.

Many sites, however, include a term or condition that links are only allowed where they are to the home page (so that those who have paid to advertise on the home page are not annoyed and circumvented).

Further information

A site with some of the best links to other ecommerce legal sites, particularly in the USA, is the European Commission's at: <http://bscw2.ispo.cec.be/ecommerce/Welcome.html>. It has a very good 'Links' section.

Further information on the EU jurisdiction regulation is on the DTI Website at <http://www.dti.gov.uk/cacp/ca/ecommerce.htm>. Comments should be sent to Martin Bond, Consumer Affairs Directorate, DTI, 1 Victoria St, London SW1H 0ET, e-mail: <martin.bond@dti.gsi.gov.uk>. The DTI has issued its own guidance on the regulation, which came into force in March 2002 – 'Guidance Note Cross Border Consumer Contractual Disputes: Guidance on the Rules on Jurisdiction and Applicable Law' – available at: <http://www.dti.gov.uk/CACP/ca/policy/jurisdiction/index/htm>.

The Website of the UK Information Commissioner contains all the materials referred to here. It can be found at: <http://www.dataprotection.gov.uk>. The section on the Data Protection Act 1998 contains the relevant details. It includes a copy of the general Introduction to the Act and the transborder data flow materials described in this chapter, including the 'International Transfers of Personal Data: Advice on Compliance with the 8th Data Protection Principle' document of the Commission (<http://www.dataprotection.gov.uk/intransf8.htm>).

The Code of Practice 'For users of CCTV' under the 1998 Act is available at: <http://www.dataprotection.gov.uk/cctvcop.htm>.

A full listing of every business which has registered under the Act can be found at <http://www.dpr.gov.uk>. This is a useful site for checking whether businesses are registered or not.

All data protection regulations are published on the UK government statutory instruments Website at <http://www.legislation.hmso.gov.uk> under 'Statutory Instruments'. Some of the more recent ones bear SI numbers 2000/413–419 and 183–206.

The Confederation of British Industry has produced model terms which could be included in contracts which would need the adequacy test under the Act. The CBI Website is at: <http://www.cbi.org.uk>.

Details of lawyers specializing in this field are in the Chambers & Partners directory at <http://www.chambersandpartners.com>.

Tolley's *Data Protection Handbook*, a text book on the 1998 Act by Susan Singleton (2002).

The Advertising Standards Authority in the UK operates the British Codes of Advertising and Sales Promotion (new versions came into force on 1 October 1999). The codes can be obtained by telephoning (+44) (0)20 7580 5555, or see the Website at: <http://www.asa.org.uk>.

Osborne Clark solicitors run a marketing law Website at: <http://www.marketinglaw.co.uk>.

A useful Website on US advertising law can be found at: <http://www.arentfox.com/quickGuide/businessLines/advert/advertisingLaw/advertisinglaw.html>.

Regulation 44/2001 of 22 December 2000 'on jurisdiction and the recognition and enforcement of judgements in civil and commercial matters' is published at OJ 16.1.2001 L121.

4 CONTRACTING ON THE INTERNET

This chapter looks at the formation of contracts on the Internet. In particular, it examines legislation in this area, including the new laws on electronic signatures and distance selling. It does not provide a full description of English or any other jurisdiction's contract law. It is usually sensible to talk through an Internet contracting proposal with a solicitor, even if only for a few minutes, to ensure there are no difficult contract issues with what is proposed, as every selling situation varies. Chapter 5 examines negotiation of contracts using e-mail, and what to do when contract and other situations 'go wrong'.

Most important of all, the business selling over the Internet needs to ensure that the terms and conditions do actually apply between the parties. If the terms, however well drawn up, are rejected by the buyer or never sent to the buyer at all, then they are of no legal use.

Forming a contract

Under English law, contracts are mostly formed verbally. Whenever goods are bought in a shop or ordered by telephone, no one questions whether a binding contract is in place. Of course there is. It is the same with e-mail. In fact, it is easier to prove an e-mail transaction. It is easier to show that terms and conditions were accepted (when the buyer clicked to indicate that they were) than it would be with a telephone order.

English law is therefore ideally placed to be used for Internet transactions. There are some very rare areas of law where a signature is needed on a piece of physical paper, such as where copyright is assigned or property transferred. In other cases, for example where a contract is for such a large sum or of such importance that all sides accept that even if the negotiations and drafts have all been done by e-mail, there will be a hard copy signed by all sides. However, some other EU states do not have such rules. The legal changes proposed to recognize electronic signatures are discussed later in this chapter.

CHECKLIST FOR BUSINESSES

- Do we have terms and conditions on our Website which can be viewed before people contract?
- Do the terms say who we are, our limited company name and number, and give a telephone, fax, address and other details, not just e-mail contacts?
- Should we obtain a Web trader or other approved symbol accreditation (see Chapter 5) to display on the site?
- Do we gather personal data when people register on the site or order goods such that we should display the data protection symbol (see page 40)?
- If we gather personal data, do we tell people all the details we are required by the Data Protection Act 1998 to tell them such as the purposes for which their data will be held (see Chapter 3 and <http://www.dataprotection.gov.uk>)?
- Are our delivery charges and packaging charges clear?
- Do we say how long we take to deliver goods or services?
- Do we say whether customs duties might be charged in addition?
- Do we make it clear when and how an order can be cancelled?
- By law, do we have to give people a cooling-off period to cancel (see 'Distance Contracts Directive' below)?
- For business sales, do we have proper credit-checking procedures before contracts proceed in the normal way?
- Do we need an employee Internet policy which covers who is and who is not allowed to order goods electronically on behalf of the company (see Chapter 1)?
- Have we looked at the sites of the best competitors in our sector to check that we have covered all the issues they have?
- Would it be sensible to have the terms checked by an Internet lawyer?
- Is it made absolutely clear which country's laws apply to the contract, where disputes are handled, and whether there are countries from which we do not accept orders?
- Have we complied with EU and UK competition law in any restrictions we place on the site as regards from where a customer may come, for example have we any territorial restrictions which may carve up the EU market?

Those buying over the Internet also need to consider legal issues. 'Let the buyer beware!' is a phrase that litters English contract law cases. The greatest risk for buyers is contracting on the supplier's standard terms of business, whether electronically or otherwise. It is very hard when ordering automatically over a Website to alter the supplier's conditions of sale. For business transactions, it is best to clarify first whose terms will apply. Ignoring the major contracts awarded after a lengthy tendering process, the best protection any purchaser can give itself is to draw up its own terms and conditions of purchase. These can be published on a Website. Increasingly, purchasing Websites are being set up. Buyer power can be harnessed. Large corporate groups can buy centrally. In the USA, three large car companies who have set up a buying Website are being investigated by the US anti-trust authorities (joint purchasing should always be vetted first by competition/anti-trust lawyers, in case it breaches Article 81 in the EU or the Competition Act 1998 in the UK).

Table 4.1 shows just some of the differences between the standard conditions of sale and purchase, and thus why it is important to have standard terms which favour the party concerned.

Table 4.1   Differences between standard conditions of sale and purchase

Sale	Purchase
Goods must be delivered on time: time is of the essence.	There is no liability for delay.
Goods must conform to the contract specification.	The supplier must endeavour to meet the specification.
The supplier owns the goods until payment is made.	The buyer owns the goods on delivery.
Money is paid up front, there is no right to cancel.	There are acceptance tests, rights to cancel, and payment is delayed until satisfied.

COMMON FALLACIES: CONTRACT LAW

The courts will overturn an unfair contract term
False. In very limited cases where a clause excludes liability and this is unreasonable and the clause is not negotiated, the courts may overturn it. It will cost the buyer a fortune in legal fees, and they may not win. 'Let the buyer beware' applies equally here. The courts do not act as nanny for the businessperson who suddenly realizes they have inadvertently accepted terms and conditions they should not have done. Usually, they are stuck with them, and the hapless purchasing manager may be out of a job. The excessive price, the lengthy minimum contract period, and the right of the

supplier to increase prices may all seem unreasonable terms, but they can rarely be avoided if they are in a contract.

A businessperson can get out of contract terms they did not read
False. Provided the terms were supplied to the buyer, they will apply. If the buyer was too lazy to read them, that is their fault.

The terms are not valid because the buyer did not understand them
False. The courts expect buyers either to reject terms they do not understand, or to take advice from lawyers to make sure they do understand them.

There was no contract, as nothing was signed
In English law, a contract just requires an offer, acceptance and consideration (usually an agreed price). Most contracts are made verbally, in shops, by telephone, mail order or by e-mail. Writing has never been required in the UK.

The EU Electronic Commerce Directive 2000/31 (OJ L178/1, 17 July 2000), which is due to be brought into force throughout the EU by 17 January 2002 (but the DTI are implementing it later in 2002), will force all EU member states to have similar requirements, and a directive on electronic signatures has already been agreed (Directive 1999/93, OJ L13/12, 19 January 2000) which was implemented in the UK by the Electronic Communications Act 2000.

NOTICES ON THE SITE

The Website should ideally contain the following legal elements:

- *A copyright notice, such as*: '© E.S. Singleton 2000. All Rights Reserved'. It may go on and state what people can and cannot do with material on the site, such as that they may download and print it, but not modify it or copy it in any other way, nor use it for any commercial purpose (just because material is on the Internet in the public domain does *not* mean copyright does not exist in it. Much information in the public domain is protected strictly by copyright, from newspapers to telephone directories).
- *A trade mark notice, such as*: 'The Big Duckling is a registered trade mark of BDD Ltd', or 'The Big Duckling ®'. (™ means unregistered trade mark. It is an offence to claim a mark is registered when it is not.)
- *A privacy policy* (examples of such policies appear on many Websites, including <http://www.dell.co.uk> and <http://www.dataprotection.gov.uk>).

This is particularly important if a lot of 'personal data' will be handled. 'Personal data' is defined in the Data Protection Act 1998. Further information on the Act is available at <http://www.dataprotection.gov.uk> and in Tolley's *Data Protection Handbook* a text book on the 1998 Act by Susan Singleton (2002).

- *Terms and conditions for use of the site*: These typically take two forms. If the site has a lot of content, perhaps free information, a publisher's site, software downloads or other things which may attract liability, then it is sensible to have all users 'sign' up to the terms of use of the site. In other cases, terms and conditions of sale where goods are bought online should be given. These users should have a chance to read the terms before they place their order, otherwise under contract law those conditions may not apply.
- *Corporate information*: Many Websites do not even give the business address, telephone and fax numbers of the company concerned. Under the Business Names Act 1985 and Companies Act 1985, businesses have to provide certain statutory information on business letters, invoices, and so on. It is wise to give this information on the Website, and also on e-mails.

Most Website designers will not draft privacy policies and copyright notices or other legal documents for Websites for the client. Indeed, they may often forget even to suggest them. The buyer needs to take legal advice on these matters to ascertain the extent to which it needs them, and the precise wording for such notices. Appendix 3 gives some examples of terms and conditions for a Website.

CONTRACTING WITH DESIGNERS

Some businesses design their own Websites in-house. Others use third-party designers. This section assumes the latter. In such a case, a number of important legal issues arise. These are addressed in turn.

What work is to be done?

Many companies believe they need a good Website, but have little idea of what it should contain or how it should look. However, they should draw up a statement of user requirements, or for bigger jobs put the work out to tender with a user specification or description of the work to be done, so that a number of different responses to a tender can be obtained and considered, and a comparison of price can also take place.

Some large-value public sector contracts will need to be advertised in the EU *Official Journal*, and will come within the public procurement regime of the EU/UK. In such cases, the formalities of those laws must be followed precisely. However, most Website design contracts are either in the private sector or are of relatively low value, so the public procurement rules do not apply. Although that may mean there is no compulsory tendering process, it does not mean only one possible contractor should be considered. There are obvious, sound commercial reasons why a comparison of different suppliers is sensible, in relation to Website design, as with any other services.

A difficulty for those who do not understand the technology, or indeed the Internet, is knowing what to ask for from the designer. Look at the sites of competitors and others. Of course they cannot be copied, as that would be breach of copyright, but the ideas used on them can be taken. There is no copyright in ideas, just in their expression. Thus, for example, the idea of having a Website where people can book flights and holidays at the last minute is not a copyright work. However, someone calling their site <www.lastsecond.com> would be likely to be sued for passing off and breach of trade mark by <www.lastminute.com>.

In some cases, it will be best to pay a company to provide a detailed specification, rather than commissioning work where it is not clear what work is required. However, much depends on the budget involved as to whether this is worthwhile.

From a technical point of view, this book does not provide advice. However, legally, the important thing is to ensure that the contract firmly pins down the designer as to what is to be done. There should be no discretion and no lack of clarity. Obviously, the contract can contain precise 'change control' clauses which set out what happens if the parties want to alter the agreement later, or in particular alter the scope or extent of the work. These provisions are very useful in contracts, and ensure that all changes are properly documented and signed by both parties. There is then no scope later for one party saying that a change was or was not agreed.

When is it to be done by?
The legal issue on timing is whether 'time is of the essence' (the work must be done on time, and if not, an action for damages for breach of contract may be brought), or whether the designer must simply use their reasonable endeavours to have the work done on time. The term 'best endeavours' has a special legal meaning – that 'all the stops will be pulled out', helicopters will be hired, people flown from all over the world, or whatever is necessary to have something done on time. 'Best endeavours' is a very strong obligation indeed in English law. 'Reasonable endeavours' simply means that someone must try.

Timing may not matter with some sites. With others, speed is absolutely crucial, and with several new dot.coms all fighting to get on the market first, the one which succeeds first may be the only site which succeeds.

Exclusion of liability

If the work is not done on time and there is a legal obligation to do so, the buyer can sue for damages. The sum to be claimed will depend on what the losses are. If the delay has had little effect and no loss has resulted, the buyer will not recover much, if anything. If the delay has cost many thousands of pounds, then the damages could be high. However, standard terms and conditions of designers will often exclude or limit liability. There may be a maximum sum which can be claimed if there is a delay. It may not be very high. If it is too low, the courts may, in a contract made on standard terms, find that the clause is invalid. Under the Unfair Contract Terms Act 1977, an unreasonable exclusion of liability clause will be void. Sometimes the contract will exclude liability for consequential losses, and will limit liability for direct losses or all losses under the agreement, perhaps to the contract price. Indeed, this is the standard clause in many suppliers' contracts.

For those involved with Websites, it is not always easy to know what consequential losses or other loss and damage may flow from a breach of contract. If a Website is poor, few sales will be achieved. However, objective and artistic appraisal of a site can be difficult. If the buyer has strong views about how a site should look or which features are crucial, then those features should be terms of the contract, and the supplier should be contracted to supply them. In the contract, avoid phrases such as 'try to', 'use reasonable endeavours to' or 'aim to'. Go for terms such as 'shall', 'best endeavours to' or 'achieve compliance with the specification'.

Where timing is crucial, it is wise to include a clause in the contract that if there is a delay, then a certain sum in liquidated damages is paid. This sum must not be plucked out of the air or it runs the risk of being held by a court to be a 'penalty clause'. Penalty clauses are void. They are not worth the paper they are written on. The courts like to decide what someone has lost through a breach of contract. They do not want their roles usurped by contractual parties. However, a clause which provides a genuine pre-estimate of what the actual loss will be if there is a breach of contract will be valid. Keep a piece of paper showing the calculations and how they were made, in case it has to be produced later in court in proving the estimate was genuine. Many commercial contracts include wording such as the example given on page 59.

CASE EXAMPLE

Hotel Services Ltd v. Hilton International Hotels (UK) Ltd (High Court, 15 March 2000) (not yet reported, except on <www.casetrack.co.uk>)

Facts This case involved minibars in hotel rooms. Hilton bought some minibars which it said were not of satisfactory quality or fit for their purpose. The judge begins his judgment with the words: 'In the minibar to be found in many hotel bedrooms unimagined problems lurk.' The Robobar was a device developed and marketed by HSL which electronically registered on the guest's account any use of the contents. Between 1986 and 1996, Hilton used the Robobars in a number of their hotels. The chillers leaked ammonia, which both corroded the equipment and created a risk (albeit a very small one) of injury or even fatality to guests. Repeated endeavours to correct the malfunction failed.

The clause The contract provided as follows as regards limitation of liability:

Section 14: Liability

(1) The Company [HSL] will not in any circumstances be liable for any indirect or consequential loss, damage or liability arising from any defect in or failure of the System or any part thereof or the performance of this Agreement or any breach hereof by the Company or its employees.

(2) Without prejudice to paragraph (1) above all and any liability on the Company's part arising in contract or tort (including negligence) or otherwise, howsoever, for any loss, damage, liability or injury of whatsoever nature arising in any way whatsoever from or in connection with this Agreement and/or the System and any part thereof (including without limitation the use, supply, possession, installation, repair or presence of the same) shall be limited to the net value of the System and the Company's performance of its obligations under Section 9.

(3) The limitation on and exclusions from liability contained in this Section shall not apply to or affect the Company's liability for death or personal injury caused by the negligence of the Company or its employees for which it is legally liable.

Findings It was held that where the equipment, as here, turns out to be unusable and possibly dangerous, the cost of 'putting it where it can do no harm and – if when in use it was showing a direct profit – of the consequent loss of profit' was a direct loss, and liability was not excluded.

Lessons State in contracts with designers and other suppliers which losses are direct and which are not, so that there is no doubt who is responsible for which losses if a subsequent breach of contract occurs and the exclusion of liability clause must be relied upon.

> *For each week of delay after the Delivery Date*
> *in supply of the Deliverables, the Buyer may*
> *deduct the sum of [£1,000] from the Price up*
> *to a maximum of four weeks' delay after which*
> *the Buyer may give notice to terminate the*
> *agreement forthwith under the provisions of*
> *clause [__] without prejudice to its other rights*
> *under this Agreement. The parties agree that*
> *such sum is a genuine pre-estimate of the*
> *Buyer's loss arising from such delay.*

It is not possible under English law to exclude liability for death or personal injury caused by negligence.

It is generally sensible to take legal advice from solicitors on clauses excluding and limiting liability. Do not modify such clauses in standard purchase contracts without checking first the legal effect, and also whether the buyer's insurance company will allow such a change. Some insurers, particularly of suppliers, need to see and clear the wording on contracts in this field.

Force majeure: Acts of God

The other clause to check in this respect is any clause called 'force majeure' or 'Act of God'. This may excuse delay on the part of the supplier for circumstances beyond its reasonable control. The buyer should check that such a clause does not excuse failures by third parties for whom the supplier is responsible, or industrial disputes. It is reasonable to excuse the supplier where delay is caused by riot, war, flood, government order, and so on.

Mitigating loss

A buyer presented with a breach of contract by a supplier has a legal duty to reduce or mitigate its loss. It cannot sit back, letting huge losses accumulate. The contract may, where on the supplier's standard terms, also include obligations on the buyer, for example to back up data or have its own insurance cover and disaster recovery schemes in operation. If the buyer has not complied with these provisions and suffers a greater loss because of that, then again full recovery may not be possible.

Who should do the work?

Make sure the contract is clear as to whether or not the contractor or designer is allowed to sub-contract the work. Also consider whether the contractor being used may in fact be classed as an employee of the buyer.

Take legal advice. In general, the buyer will want to know who is doing the work, and will not be happy with rights to sub-contract. Under the Contracts (Rights of Third Parties) Act 1999, which applies to contracts made from 11 May 2000, where a contract mentions a third party as a beneficiary under it, that third party may sue under the contract. The buyer may find that its contractor's sub-contractor can sue the buyer for breach of the contractor's contract with the buyer. In most cases, it will be sensible to exclude the Act.

Who should own the rights?

Designs on a Website, the layout, the drawings and pictures, and even sound or motion clips used will all be copyright works. In addition, there will be the corporate brochure-type material used, text of press releases reproduced, corporate reports, photographs of members of staff, messages sent to any bulletin boards on sites there, and in many cases computer software which runs the site, sometimes written by the designer or their colleagues. All these items are protected by copyright.

Copyright is one of the so-called 'intellectual property rights'. It is incoherent, ephemeral. Owning a book does not mean owning the copyright in the book. It is an intangible right. It is the key right on the Internet, and the principal asset of many of the leading Internet companies. It is valuable. It is also easily breached.

Copyright in the UK is protected under the Copyright, Designs and Patents Act 1988. It arises as soon as a work is created, and it is breached by copying. In most countries, it is not registered. It simply comes into being as soon as it is created. The author will own the rights in it, but they can be licensed to other people so that they may use them, usually temporarily.

Exclusive and non-exclusive licences

Licences can be exclusive or non-exclusive.

An exclusive licence means that only one licence is granted. No one else can use the copyright, even the author, unless the agreement or contract says so. A 'sole' licence is not quite the same. In law, this means that only one licence is granted, but the owner may also use the right.

An exclusive licence is not as good as ownership. First, it may be limited in time. Second, it may be revocable and terminable in certain situations. Third, it is not owned. Title to the copyright has not been transferred to the exclusive licensee.

It is better if the buyer requires by a contract term that as soon as any commissioned copyright works specially written for it are created, they will automatically vest in the buyer. An alternative is that once the buyer has paid, the rights are assigned or transferred to the buyer. That is not as good for a buyer.

The courts do not readily construe an assignment unless one is agreed. Generally, it is much better that agreement is in writing. It is hard to prove agreements made verbally, and under the Copyright, Designs and Patents

CASE EXAMPLE: OWNERSHIP OF COPYRIGHT

Andre Durand v. *Mario Molino and Mario e Peppe Ltd* ((1999) LTL 12/10/99)

The Facts Mario Molino is a restaurateur. His company commissioned the painting of a portrait of him to go on the menu covers at the restaurant 'The Four Seasons'. This was in exchange for £15,000 worth of free meals. No agreement was reached, nor was there discussion on what else the work could be used for.

The Judgment The court said the commission was commercial, to promote the restaurant and the person paying, so the commissioner could prevent others using the work.

The case followed an earlier discussion about Classic FM (*Robin Day* v. *Classic FM plc*) which had held that when trying to find out the terms of

implied licences, the courts must only find the minimum licence necessary to give effect to the arrangement, not the wide licence or even ownership right which commissioners claim in most disputes, usually unsuccessfully. If the commissioner is the subject of a portrait, the court said they had the right to control it, and the implied licence was an exclusive perpetual licence.

The artist had also produced a work called 'Pizza Diana', which depicted a pizza being given to the late Diana, Princess of Wales, which after her death the parties agreed should be altered, leading to a third work in dispute in the case. The first 'Pizza Diana' licence expressly said that the artist kept copyright, but the court said that even so, he could not withdraw the licence (there were no contract terms about this, so the court was

looking to find the implied terms). The licence extended to a right to produce greeting cards and postcards showing the work. Finally, the revised 'Pizza Diana' work had no agreement at all, so the agreement for the first such work applied. This is important for many contractual situations. Normally, the courts will go back to the last set of terms agreed if a new replacement set is not put forward. However, stationery showing the 'Pizza Diana' second version had not been licensed, and they were infringements.

Lessons The court implied copyright licence terms in this case, which in practice it would be dangerous for those using copyright works to assume. It is much better to agree the terms of any licence and ownership of rights in advance, before the work is produced.

Act 1988, copyright must be assigned by agreement in writing (the new electronic signatures laws described in Chapter 5 will alter this requirement to allow certain digital or electronic signatures). An agreement which says who will own copyright as soon as it is created – that is, it will first *vest* in the buyer – is not an assignment at all. An agreement which says that copyright will be owned by the designer and will be transferred or assigned to the buyer later, such as when payment is made, will be an assignment. Legal advice should be sought on these matters.

Under the Copyright, Designs and Patents Act 1988, it is also possible for copyright to be owned jointly, but this can be complicated and is not ideal.

Practical points

Sometimes designers with the toughest, most professional approach to their terms and conditions may be the best to use. The small outfit which accepts the buyer's stringent purchase terms and conditions may know that they could easily liquidate their company if a claim occurred, so you should not always decide whom to use solely on the basis of which supplier offers the buyer the best legal conditions. The legal conditions are just one of the reasons for a particular choice of supplier. However, some obligations are too important to risk a one-sided legal contract. Even low-value Web contracts can lead to huge losses for the buyer if things go wrong, so do a careful risk analysis, arrange backups, and take out appropriate insurance.

Areas of law

The most important principle of English law for buyers is that the express terms written in a contract or set of terms and conditions will prevail over most other English laws. Unlike some Continental jurisdictions, the contract prevails in English and US and other 'common law' jurisdictions, so:

- Read contracts.
- Negotiate contracts.
- Understand contracts.
- Change unacceptable terms.
- Do not take deliveries or place purchase orders until contract terms are agreed.

Areas of law to consider include the following.

SALE OF GOODS ACT 1979

This implies terms into contracts for sale of goods that goods are of satisfactory quality and fit for their purpose.

Most suppliers' contracts exclude this.

The exclusion usually works. If it is 'unreasonable' and in a standard form contract, it may be subject to challenge under the Unfair Contract Terms Act 1977.

Buyers are better off negotiating strict service-level agreements, specifications, statements of user requirements or other provisions stating exactly what the goods will do.

SUPPLY OF GOODS AND SERVICES ACT 1982

This says that services will be performed with due skill and care.

It is even harder to show that this has been breached. Again with services, have contractual requirements about standards of service which are detailed and precise and are *part of the contract*. Make any important statements part of the contract. If they are not, they will have little validity.

COMPETITION LAW

Watch out for agreements with competitors about prices and markets. Make sure agreements such as distribution and franchising contracts, patent and know-how licences, joint ventures, and so on are checked out for compliance with detailed EU and UK regulations.

Many contracts are drafted to take account of the EU exemption regulations. On 1 June 2000, Regulation 2790/1999 came into force which affects 'vertical' agreements such as distribution contracts. Many contracts will need to be checked again.

The rules prohibit both anti-competitive agreements and abuse of market power by dominant undertakings.

Breach of EU and UK competition law can lead to fines of 10 per cent of turnover.

Check the Office of Fair Trading Website at <http://www.oft.gov.uk> for supply details on the Competition Act 1998, which came in to force on 1 March 2000.

Check the European Commission's Website at <http://www.europa.eu. int>.

Report breaches of competition law to the Office of Fair Trade and Commission. Businesses and consumers have a right to sue for damages for breach of these statutes.

Remember that buyers, too, can breach the rules. Watch out for collective purchasing arrangements which restrict you from buying outside the group.

PUBLIC PROCUREMENT

Are the public sector or utilities involved? If so, the public procurement rules may apply. Those affected usually know all about the public procurement rules in the EU/UK.

Make sure large-value contracts are advertised in the EU *Official Journal* when these rules apply. Avoid post-tender negotiation. Follow all the strict rules for tendering.

COMMERCIAL AGENTS

In the EU, commercial agents are protected. In the UK, the EU agency directive is implemented by the Commercial Agents (Council Directive) Regulations 1993.

If an agent is sacked, they can claim substantial compensation. Many Internet contracts involve agency, and the level of ignorance of the 1993 regulations, particularly in this sector, is appalling. Butterworths' *Commercial Agency Agreement: Law and Practice* by Susan Singleton (1998) is a book which covers the regulations in detail.

INTELLECTUAL PROPERTY

The buyer needs to know that the goods do not breach the copyright, patents, designs or trade marks of a third party. Reference should be made to Chapter 3, which covers intellectual property rights in detail.

Make sure the contract contains appropriate warranties. Take advice before importing, particularly from outside the EEA, even genuine products, as the law is complex.

DATA PROTECTION

The purchaser may be handling personal data about individuals. If that is the case, they should register under the Data Protection Act 1998 in the UK, which came into force on 1 March 2000.

Details of the Act are on the Website of the UK Information Commissioner at <www.dataprotection.gov.uk>. Data protection was addressed in Chapter 3, particularly in the context of the Internet and export of goods.

FORMING A CONTRACT: POINTS TO WATCH

- Make sure the conditions of purchase are given to the supplier by e-mail or by some other means.
- State that only business on those terms is accepted.
- Make sure that the terms are also on the purchase order, whether it is sent electronically or not.
- If the supplier sends their conditions back, reject them.
- Keep rejecting them – the one who gets in last wins in the 'battle of the forms', as such a dispute is called.
- For bigger contracts, negotiate the terms.

ENFORCING THE CONTRACT

Businesses should make sure they enforce their legal rights, or they may lose the right to do so. Always take action, even if only by sending a short holding letter, if a breach comes to light. Consider the following points:

- Keep close watch on breaches of contract.
- Reject defective goods immediately.
- Do not accept goods until tested.
- Do not let breaches of contract pass, or rights can be waived.
- Document in writing what has gone wrong – in court cases, the side with the best documents often wins.
- Follow the escalation/dispute-resolution procedures in the contract to the letter.

WHERE DO DISPUTES GO?

Most big companies do not go to court. They know better. The English legal system is the envy of many countries of the world. Vast areas have modelled themselves on our system. It is good, but it does not come cheap. A complex commercial or intellectual property dispute in the High Court in London rarely costs less than £100,000 (a currency converter can be found at <http://www.xe.net/currency>).

It is therefore not surprising that most disputes are settled out of court. Lawyers, judges, even the Civil Procedure Rules encourage settlement at every turn. Go away and mediate. If the matter does reach court, you can then show what steps have been taken to settle the matter.

Sometimes the contract will specify that disputes go to formal arbitration. This can be just as expensive. Usually, solicitors and barristers are involved. However, proceedings are held in secret.

In other cases, an informal attempt at mediation or alternative dispute-resolution (ADR) is tried first, although this cannot be guaranteed to succeed (see Chapter 5 for more on this).

These basic buying and selling law issues should be considered for all transactions. The rest of this chapter considers particular laws which apply to electronic commerce.

Electronic Commerce Directive

Under current English law, a contract is made when an offer is accepted for which there is consideration (normally money, or money's worth). The Electronic Commerce Directive (Directive 2000/31, 8 June 2000, OJ L178/1, 17 July 2000) is relevant here. As well as dealing with liability of Internet service providers (as covered in Chapter 1), it looks at contract-formation. It requires minimum information to be provided to buyers, such as the name of the supplier and their address.

It says that unsolicited e-mails must be clearly identified as such. (See also the Distance Selling Directive 97/7, discussed on page 74.) Article 9 provides that member states must ensure that their legal systems allow contracts to be concluded by electronic means. It provides in Article 10 that for consumer contracts, people are told comprehensively and unambiguously and before an order is placed:

a the different technical steps to follow to conclude a contract
b whether the contract will be filed by the service provider, and whether it will be accessible
c the technical means for identifying and correcting input errors prior to placing an order
d the languages offered for conclusion of the contract.

Contract terms and general conditions must be made available in a way that allows the recipient to store and reproduce them.

Article 11 deals with placing an order. It says that:

– the service provider must acknowledge receipt of the recipient's order without undue delay and by electronic means
– the order and the acknowledgement of receipt are deemed to be received when the parties to whom they are addressed are able to access them.

Electronic signatures and the Electronic Communication Act 2000

Both the EU and the UK now have, or are about to have, legislation which allows an 'electronic' signature to have legal validity. The UK legislation is in the Electronic Communications Act 2000. The Act defines an electronic signature as:

> Anything in electronic form as –
>
> (a) is incorporated into or otherwise logically associated with any electronic communication or electronic data; and
> (b) purports to be so incorporated or associated for the purpose of being used in establishing the authenticity of the communication or data, the integrity of the communication or data, or both.

Section 7(3) also requires that there must be an accompanying statement which confirms that the signature, a means of producing, communicating or verifying the signature, or a procedure applied to the signature is 'a valid means of establishing the authenticity of the communication or data, the integrity of the communication or data, or both'. For the layperson, an electronic signature will be an independently verified electronic means of proving that a document has been signed by a particular person. This section explores some of the implications arising from these measures. There are two principal points:

1. Electronic signatures are likely to result in cost savings. Printing out and signing documents simply for the purposes of signature is time-consuming and largely pointless.
2. However, businesses need certainty in legal matters, so the legislative protections assured at EU and UK level must be sufficient to make a company decide on an informed basis that it is happy as a result to move fully to ecommerce.

The European Commission has adopted a directive guaranteeing EU-wide recognition of electronic signatures (Directive 1999/93). In some EU states, only hand-written signatures have been legally valid, but this legislation extends that recognition to electronic signatures, and applies the Internal Market principles of free movement of services and home country control to ecommerce.

In England, legal agreements are made when an offer is accepted for which there is consideration. Scotland has a different legal system which is not identical in all respects. In England, a contract can be made verbally, as happens every time goods are bought in a shop or by telephone by mail order through a call centre. E-mail makes the formation of such contracts even more certain and clear. The nightmare for the contracts manager dealing with telephone orders has been how to communicate complex terms and conditions to customers in time before contracts are made, and how to ensure there is a clear, provable trail as to when and if a contract was formed, and what was agreed when.

All those problems are swept away with orders received by e-mail. Customers can even be technically prohibited from moving to the next stage of the ordering process until they accept the supplier's terms of business. A full record of what was agreed is available electronically, and can be produced if a dispute arises.

There remain only a few areas of English law where a 'signature' is required on a piece of paper. For example, assigning copyright requires a signature in writing, as do many land transactions. The government has ambitious targets for allowing contact with it and official filings to be achieved by this means, but these have not all yet been achieved. Usually, the requirement for a signature is in areas where complete certainty is needed. For example, it may not matter if Janice in purchasing has ordered ten packs of A4 paper by telephone or e-mail, perhaps even if this exceeds her authority, but it is crucial that the contract to lease the new headquarters building is not signed by a property manager without the sanction of the board. In fact, a paper signature does not get round the problem of employees exceeding their authority but the company remaining bound. However, in practice, having a formal signature session removes some of those risks, and there are concerns that electronic signatures could be more easily forged than would be the case if a document were mailed by post for signature by the other party.

The European Commission says that the 'new directive constitutes an important element in the Commission's on-going efforts to drive forward the rapid development of electronic commerce so as to capitalize on its potential to generate business and create jobs. This framework provides the security that the market for online transactions demands and strengthens the EU's position in the face of international competition in this new global market.' Internal Market Commissioner Frits Bolkestein noted that the legislation is a foretaste of how the Commission intends to help develop the whole area of electronic commerce: 'We can expect half of the European population to be connected to the Internet by 2005 and our integrated approach to electronic commerce – an effective mix of government regulation and self-regulation that allows for technological development – is designed to put Europe in the forefront of this revolution.'

Electronic signatures allow someone receiving data over electronic networks, such as over the Internet, to determine the origin of the data and to check that the data has not been altered. The directive is not designed to regulate everything in detail, but defines the requirements for electronic signature certificates and certification services so as to ensure minimum levels of security and allow their free movement throughout the Internal Market.

The principal provisions are as follows.

LEGAL RECOGNITION

The directive provides that an electronic signature cannot be legally discriminated against solely on the grounds that it is in electronic form. If a certificate and the service provider as well as the signature product used meet a set of specific requirements, there will be an automatic assumption that any resulting electronic signatures are as legally valid as a hand-written signature. Moreover, they can be used as evidence in legal proceedings.

Article 5 provides that:

> *Member states shall ensure that advanced*
> *electronic signatures which are based on a*
> *qualified certificate and which are created by a*
> *secure-signature-creation device:*
>
> (a) *satisfy the legal requirements of a signature*
>   *in relation to data in electronic form in the*
>   *same manner as a handwritten signature*
>   *satisfies those requirements in relation to*
>   *paper-based data; and*
> (b) *are admissible as evidence in legal proceed-*
>   *ings.*

Member states are not allowed to deny an electronic signature legal effec-
tiveness and admissibility as evidence in legal proceedings solely on the
grounds that it is in electronic form, not based on a qualified certificate, or
not based on a qualified certificate issued by an accredited certification-
service-provider or not created by a secure-signature-creation device. The
Electronic Communications Act 2000 confirms this.

FREE CIRCULATION

All products and services related to electronic signatures can circulate freely
and are only subject to the legislation and control by the country of origin.
Member states cannot make the provision of services related to electronic
signatures subject to mandatory licensing.

LIABILITY

The legislation establishes minimum liability rules for service providers,
which would, in particular, be liable for the validity of a certificate's content.
This approach ensures the free movement of certificates and certification
services within the Internal Market, builds consumer trust, and stimulates
operators to develop secure systems and signatures without restrictive and
inflexible regulation.

A TECHNOLOGY-NEUTRAL FRAMEWORK

Given the pace of technological innovation, the legislation provides for legal
recognition of electronic signatures irrespective of the technology used (for
example, digital signatures using asymmetric cryptography or biometrics).

SCOPE

The legislation covers the supply of certificates to the public aimed at identifying the sender of an electronic message. In accordance with the principles of party autonomy and contractual freedom, it does, however, permit the operation of schemes governed by private law agreements such as corporate intranets or banking systems, where a relation of trust already exists and there is no obvious need for regulation.

INTERNATIONAL DIMENSION

In order to promote a global market in electronic commerce, the legislation includes mechanisms for co-operation with third countries on the basis of mutual recognition of certificates and on bilateral and multilateral agreements.

TIMING

The directive must be implemented by national laws by 19 July 2001 throughout the EU. The UK implemented it by the Electronic Communications Act 2000. Many EU states are keen to move forward in this area. It looks good politically to be legislating for ecommerce. In practice, for most contracts, many of which are arranged on standard terms and conditions of either sale or purchase, no signatures are required in any event under English law, so the position will not alter. There is nothing to stop a business now moving further into the ecommerce field, but it remains safer for larger contracts which are currently 'signed' by both parties to be signed in person, even if in law no signature at all would suffice without jeopardizing the validity of that deal.

In commercial practice, the electronic signature is not essential, and is unlikely to have a major effect because contracts do not have to be signed under English law anyway. However, it is a development which those involved in this area should watch.

Importing by e-mail

Most goods cannot be imported 'by e-mail'. E-mail may be the means of placing the order, and it works very well, but the goods themselves have to be shipped by conventional methods. Indeed, there are new ebusinesses setting up to deal with the logistics of e-mail deliveries. In the days of the American goldrush, a handful of gold diggers made a fortune, as are now a handful of those with dot.com ideas, but it was those running the infra-structure – the saloon bars, the railways – who almost universally made money. Much the same is true today. Logistics may appear dirty and old-fashioned, but it is the key to exporting, whether sales are by traditional means or e-mail. Of course, infrastructure in relation to e-mail also covers all the nuts and bolts of an ecommerce business, from demand for Internet legal advice to those who license and run the software systems which underpin it.

The importer operating via ecommerce where the goods are shipped by traditional methods needs effective distribution channels. The more suc-cessful Websites selling goods direct to consumers, or indeed businesses, are those which ship quickly. This is harder to achieve where goods are brought in from abroad. However, this section looks at importing by e-mail – the products/services themselves are shipped electronically. The customer normally pays by credit card via the Internet before the shipment takes place, rather than being invoiced later. Examples cover a wide range of goods and services:

1. Stephen King published a short book first on the Internet. Lines were jammed, as it proved tremendously popular, and many orders were placed.
2. Computer software is a common purchase which is then downloaded electronically once payment has been made.
3. Legal contracts can be ordered from <http://www.desktoplawyer.net>, including the much-publicized recent pre-nuptial agreement and the £60 Internet divorce papers.
4. Access to many well-known journals is now available online for subscrib-ers.
5. Some famous pop singers have started releasing their new songs on the Internet, which are downloaded for payment.
6. A condition of subscription to Sky's digital TV service is that subscribers keep the TV plugged into the telephone line, to enable them to download particular programmes on a pay TV basis or to order goods via the e-mail facility provided and allow transactions to be logged and payment details taken.
7. Offshore placing of bets is an area where there has been massive recent changes and urgent government action to stem loss of duty.
8. Ordering of pornography is the most common use of the Internet, and some is legal under English law and some illegal.
9. Share dealing – perhaps, effectively, importing financial services – is the second most common use of the Internet.

Some of these examples are not necessarily imports. The supplier might be in the UK, but it might not be. Much depends on the nature of the importer's goods/services as to whether an electronic import is possible. The legal issues which then arise are fascinating. Can traders purchase a remote island in a region with no taxes and ship their services from there, paying no profit on the taxes and avoiding all duties? The authorities are sufficiently concerned about possible avoidance of tax that learned papers have been written in many countries about how tax could be moved to consumption (purchase) more than profit, or perhaps levied on the Internet Service Provider in some way, in the same way that the European Commission has been trying for many years to levy a duty on blank audio tapes to recoup the losses of those suffering through piracy.

A few of the principal legal areas are considered below.

INTELLECTUAL PROPERTY

Where the goods are software, music, art works, journals, books, and so on, the works themselves will be protected by the intellectual property rights called 'copyright'. In most countries, this is an unregistered right and arises as soon as the work is made. Those importing works protected by copyright should seek to obtain a written assurance from the supplier in their conditions of contract that the goods do not infringe copyright in the country of import. The UK importer does not want to find, after arranging import, that there is a nasty copyright dispute going on at the High Court in London over that which is imported. Under the Copyright, Designs and Patents Act 1988, importing without consent of the UK copyright owner is an infringement of the Act.

The Publishers' Association suggested in press articles that importing books from the USA, for example, without consent of the UK copyright owner breached copyright even if the owner had sold them in the USA. This is because there is legal doubt about whether 'rights are internationally exhausted'. This international exhaustion of rights may sound complicated, but it is important that the importer grasps its effect.

Company A sells goods with a famous trade mark, FFFF, on them in the USA at $10. People in the UK have more money or are more gullible. A is able to sell the goods with the same trade mark in the UK for £20. Parallel importer C buys in the USA, imports into the UK and sells for £15. The UK distributors are furious. A is not pleased either. A sues Parallel Importer C for infringement of trade mark. A probably wins under current law, certainly after a case called *Silhouette*. There may be a single market in the

EU/EEA under European law, but not over the world. Tesco is fighting a similar case in the European Court which may result in a change, and the English courts have been critical, including in a case called *Davidoff*, but even that has had to be referred to the European Court of Justice for a decision.

This leaves the importer from outside the EEA with the difficulty of needing consent of the UK trade mark or copyright owner. The EU cases described above only apply to trade marks, so it is probably easier to import copyright, but the law is unclear and UK trade mark owners not wanting such an import can refer to the clear wording in the Copyright, Designs and Patents Act 1988 that imports to the UK require a licence or permission from the UK copyright owner.

The UK importer should therefore seek warranties from its foreign supplier about intellectual property rights, and an 'indemnity' (agreement to pay costs and damages) if such a legal action results.

CONTRACTS

A UK importer importing electronically will need to ensure it is clear whether the purchase is on the supplier's terms and conditions of supply, or the buyer's conditions of purchase. It may not technically be possible to order goods from a Website and reject the conditions of the supplier and still proceed to the shopping basket/checkout (indeed, in almost all cases it is not). So importers wanting to do business on their standard terms of purchase may need to use other means.

TAX

There is no exemption from import/customs duties for such imports. It may be harder for Customs to track down the goods as having been imported, but that does not change the legal position. Customs duties under the Community Customs Tariff (CCT) are charged on goods imported into the EU. Much depends on the nature of software imported as to whether it is classed as goods or services, and thus outside the provisions.

For those with an interest in tax, the following will be of use:

● The Organization for Economic Cooperation and Development (OECD) has developed a Taxation Framework for Electronic Commerce – see <http://www.oecd.org>.

- The Fabian Society has published a paper on this field, *Net Effect* (<http://www.fabian-society.org.uk>).
- In March 2000, the Institute of Directors published a report on the tax implications of ecommerce which can be downloaded free from: <http://www.iod.co.uk/free_policy_order.html>.

GENERAL

Import by e-mail is simple, cheap and legally effective. It can make it easier to impose conditions of supply on buyers, who have to click to indicate acceptance of terms and conditions in a way it is much harder to achieve by telephone orders and the traditional 'battle of the forms'. Businesses can avoid expensive distribution networks. They can eliminate the margins paid to many intermediate dealers and wholesalers and agents. Sales to direct consumers can easily be achieved.

Buying online

Chapter 1 described some of the hallmarking schemes for Websites which have been set up to give users assurances that the sites provide the basic information necessary so that consumers know how and for what they are contracting.

The TrustUK hallmark is part of an industry drive to self-regulation. It is the first of what are likely to be several such schemes. Accreditation will cost from £1,000–5,000 per year, and those using the symbol will comply with a code dealing with matters such as returns and pricing.

Further details are on the Website <http://www.trustuk.org.uk>.

Distance selling regulations

In 1997, the European Commission adopted Directive 97/7 – the Directive on the Protection of Consumers in Respect of Distance Contracts. The directive harmonizes the law where goods or services are bought by 'remote methods'. This is an important area of law which those selling online need to consider when they sell to customers. It does not apply if they just sell to other businesses. This area is to be contrasted with purchases in a shop, where the contract is not made by any distance methods at all, and so would not be covered by the directive. The EU member states had until 4 June 2000 to implement the directive, but the UK was very late, not doing so until 31 October 2000.

CONSUMER PROTECTION (DISTANCE SELLING) REGULATIONS 2000

The Consumer Protection (Distance Selling) Regulations 2000 implement Directive 97/7 in the UK from 31 October 2000. They were published on 31 August 2000. The final text of the regulations is on the DTI Website, and they are SI 2000/2334. The DTI has published a short guide for business which sets out the main features of the regulations and is designed to help businesses, and especially small businesses, to check that they will be ready from when the regulations come into force. The full text of the directive on distance selling on which they are based is available at: <http://europa.eu.int/eur-lex/en/lif/dat/1997/en_397L0007.html>.

The directive and the regulations cover both contracts for the supply of goods and for the supply of services concluded at a distance between suppliers acting in a commercial or professional capacity, and consumers (defined in Article 2 of the directive and Regulation 3 of the regulations as natural persons acting for purposes outside their trade, business or profession).

A distance contract is one where supplier and consumer do not come face to face up to and including the moment at which the contract is concluded (for example, mail order, telephone sales, electronic commerce). Conclusion of the contract refers to the making of the contract, rather than the time when its performance is completed. Transactions under which the seller makes initial contact at a distance but completes the contract face to face are not distance contracts.

Financial services are excluded. They will be subject to a separate directive which is not yet agreed.

APPLICATION OF THE DISTANCE SELLING DIRECTIVE/ REGULATIONS

The directive applies to most sectors of industry, even the renting of property, although it does not apply to construction contracts or sale of property. Some sectors are excluded, such as from Articles 4, 5, 6 and 7(1) for deliveries of goods for every-day consumption, where the goods are supplied by employees making regular rounds, and for accommodation, transport and leisure, where the supplier undertakes to provide these services on a specific date or within a specific period. One-off occasional distance transactions are not covered.

SCHEDULE 1 OF THE DRAFT REGULATIONS

Schedule 1 to the regulations provides a list of means of distance communication, though it is not necessarily exhaustive.

1. unaddressed printed matter
2. addressed printed matter
3. letter
4. press advertising with order form
5. catalogue
6. telephone with human intervention
7. telephone without human intervention (automatic calling machine, audio text)
8. radio
9. videophone (telephone with screen)
10. electronic mail
11. facsimile machine (fax)
13. television (teleshopping).

NO APPLICATION TO SALES TO BUSINESSES

The regulations and directive do *not* apply to business-to-business communications, so the first issue every business has to address is whether it makes direct sales to consumers or not. Assuming it does, it then needs to determine whether it uses any 'distance' means. Shops mostly will not, whereas mail order, digital/satellite TV ordering, telesales and Internet shopping clearly do. All the posted junk mail consumers receive is, of course, also caught. It is not, however, banned. It is simply regulated, as provided below.

INFORMATION TO BE PROVIDED

Consumers must be provided with certain information under Article 4.1 of the directive and Regulations 7 and 8 of the regulations, clearly and comprehensively, and on time. The DTI describe this as fairly basic: name and address of supplier (a PO box address is not enough), main characteristics of goods or services, price, arrangements for payment, existence of right of withdrawal where this exists, information on aftersales and guarantees, and so on. The existing Mail Order Transactions (Information) Order 1976 (SI 1976/1812) covers some but not all of the necessary information, and does not apply to all of the types of transaction covered by the directive. The regulations repeal that order (by Regulation 2).

WRITTEN CONFIRMATION

The information should be provided in 'another durable medium available and accessible to him' by the time of delivery at the latest. In the case of services, the confirmation should be provided in good time during the performance of the contract. There are some exemptions for things such as gifts. The DTI think that e-mail is fine for this purpose where the consumer has placed the order by e-mail in the first place.

Indeed, many Internet ordering services provide much more useful contractual and company information than many mail order operations. The user can download and/or print the full order details and check online at any point for the status of their order.

CANCELLATION OF CONTRACTS

Consumers have the right to cancel contracts within seven working days without penalty and without giving any reason (Regulations 10, 11 and 12). The period starts from the date of receipt in the case of goods, and the date of the conclusion of the contract in the case of services (or the date when written confirmation was received, if this was later). The date of the conclusion of the contract is the date when the contract is made, rather than the date on which performance is completed. Where the right to cancel applies, the only charge that may be made to consumers is the cost of return post in the case of goods. The period is 3 months if certain information is not given to the consumer on time.

Not all contracts can be cancelled, such as those where the services have already started before the cancellation period is over, or where the goods or services' price is dependent on fluctuations in the financial market, contracts to consumers' specifications or customized, or for the supply of video or audio records or computer software which is unsealed by the consumer. The exceptions to the cancellation right are set out in Article 13. Some computer software is supplied online and not unsealed at all, and it is unfortunate there is no definition of unsealing. Software suppliers for downloading online therefore do not know whether a right to cancel exists or not.

MONEY BACK

If contracts are cancelled, the consumer must be reimbursed money paid. The consumer can be charged for the cost of return post in the case of goods. Reimbursement must be made within 30 days of exercising the cancellation right.

CREDIT AGREEMENTS

Where a consumer cancels, any related credit agreement is cancelled (Article 15). In 1997, the DTI implemented a similar provision in the Timeshare Directive, and imposed a requirement in the Timeshare Regulations 1997 (SI 1997/1081) that the vendor notify the credit provider if the consumer withdraws from the contract.

Orders must be executed within 30 days (Regulation 19). If not, money should be returned.

SUBSTITUTING GOODS

Member states can allow sellers to substitute goods for those ordered if consumers are told in advance that this might happen. Often with mail order, consumers are asked to indicate a second choice. The legal position is therefore unlikely to change in the UK in this respect.

CANCELLATIONS AND REFUNDS

Section 84 of the UK Consumer Credit Act removes any liability of the debtor under a regulated consumer credit agreement where their credit card is used by another person not acting as their agent (fraudulent use). Section 84 states that the cardholder may be made liable to the extent of £50 where the card is out of the possession of an authorized person (that is, lost or stolen). Further, if another person obtains the card with the consent of the debtor, the liability of the cardholder is unlimited. Once a cardholder has given oral or written notice to the creditor that the card has been lost or stolen or is liable to misuse, the cardholder then ceases to be liable for any loss suffered after notice is given. In addition, the UK Banking Code of Practice provides that the card issuer will bear the full costs for all unauthorized use of the card once the cardholder has told them that the card is stolen, and imposes a £50 maximum liability in the event of misuse before the cardholder informs them. However, this code is entirely voluntary.

Regulation 21(5) of the new regulations disapplies part of Section 84. The directive provides that where there is fraudulent use of the card, the cardholder will have *no* liability, not even for £50, so this is changed for distance contracts.

INERTIA SELLING

For those with an interest in unsolicited selling, Regulation 24 is the provision to consider. It deals with the supply of unsolicited goods and services where supply involves a demand for payment. It also exempts the consumer from the 'provision of any consideration' in cases of unsolicited supply. The DTI believes that this means that the consumer is under no obligation to keep the goods safe or enable the supplier to retrieve them.

E-MAIL

Article 10.2 of the directive provides that methods of distance selling other than faxes and automated calling machines may only be used where there is no clear objection from the consumer. The means of communication concerned include e-mail, as well as telephone and mail delivered by post. Options include an opt-in or an opt-out system.

This covers unsolicited e-mails sent by businesses to consumers for the purposes of distance selling contracts under the directive. Business-to-business e-mails are not covered. Nor does the directive cover all contracts. Financial service contracts are excluded, and will be covered under a separate directive.

The directive defines a consumer as 'any natural person who, in contracts covered by this Directive, is acting for purposes which are outside his trade, business or profession'. The type of e-mail will determine whether the recipient has been sent it in the capacity of a consumer. An e-mail sent to someone at work about a business conference is clearly a business e-mail. One sent to them about family holidays at a resort would not be.

The UK regulations do not deal with this. The government has decided that voluntary codes will be used for 'spam'.

CODES FOR ECOMMERCE

The UK government is seeking to develop:

● additional core principles to meet consumer concerns about ecommerce which will be developed further by the AEB and other bodies that issue ecommerce codes; these concerns include how consumers can avoid unsolicited e-mail

- a new body, with the working title of TrustUK, to accredit ecommerce codes that also accord with the core principles for codes described above
- a 'hallmark' that accredited codes may use on their Websites or incorporate into their logos
- the use of existing links to establish international complaints handling networks
- a way to market the ecommerce hallmark internationally
- work with the EU Commission to encourage the development of an EU-wide code
- work with the OECD on its guidelines for consumer protection in ecommerce.

Businesses marketing to consumers should watch these developments closely.

This aims to ensure the government's aim that the UK provides the best environment in the world for electronic trading, as well as reducing the problems for consumers of unsolicited bulk e-mails.

Opting in or out?

The EU Electronic Commerce Directive is neutral on opt-in or opt-out, leaving the Distance Selling Directive to regulate this. However, where member states permit such e-mail, the Electronic Commerce Directive 2000/31 (8 June 2000, OJ L178/1, 17 July 2000) requires them to ensure that service providers established on their territory make unsolicited e-mail clearly identifiable as such as soon as it shows up in the recipient's in-tray, in recognition of the additional communication costs of the recipient and the need to promote responsible filtering initiatives by industry. In 2001 the Commission held hearings on internet privacy and suggested mass e-mail mailings should only be allowed where consumers 'opt in', rather than simply fail to opt out. The Direct Marketing Association has described the plans as unworkable.

FAXES AND AUTOMATED CALLING MACHINES

The directive stipulates that prior consent is required for use of automated calling machines and faxes by suppliers. Article 12 requires prior consent for the use of fax or automated calling machines for direct marketing purposes. This is similar to the Telecommunications Data Protection Directive now implemented in the UK.

RIGHTS TO OBJECT

Mail, telephone and other means of distance communication should only be used where there is no objection from the consumer. This will require preference services, including a new e-mail preference service. It is not yet clear whether opting in or opting out will be required, as mentioned above.

Member states must allow public bodies, consumer organizations and/or professional organizations to take action under national law to ensure that the provisions of the directive are applied. The DTI proposes to follow a similar approach to the Unfair Terms in Consumer Contracts Regulations 1999, which came into force in October 1999, and allow the Consumers' Association and other bodies to bring representative actions.

Member states must make provisions to ensure that the consumer cannot contract out of or waive the rights conferred by the directive.

Further information

The DTI has lots of information on its Website: <http://www.dti.gov.uk>.

Detailed Web design agreements can be purchased from solicitors Sprecher Grier Halberstam via their Website: <http://www.weblaw.co.uk>, or from Sprecher Grier Halberstam, Lincoln House, 300 High Holborn, London WC1V 7JH. tel. 020 7544 5555, fax 020 7544 5565, e-mail <law@weblaw.co.uk>.

Bitlaw provides access to some free precedent agreements, mostly US, on Internet law: <http://www.bitlaw.com>.

Solicitors who can draw up customized Website design agreements include those in the computer law section of the Chambers and Partners Directory on the Internet at: <http:www.chambersandpartners.com>.

INTERNET AND WEB-RELATED FORMS COLLECTION 2000

It is very hard to obtain copies of Internet contracts and forms. It is therefore not surprising that the world's largest computer legal body – The Computer Law Association (<http://www.cla.org>) – found its most successful publication was the *Internet Forms Collection*. The new edition is sold as a book and with accompanying CD-ROM at US$150 for non-members. They can be ordered from the CLA Website. The forms include:

- Website development and services
- Web services transaction processing
- Service provided reseller
- Company policy statements
- Software licences
- Term of site use
- Forums and chat rooms
- Advertising
- End user Web access
- Electronic journal access
- Multimedia development.

The EU Directive is Directive 1999/93, 'A Community Framework for Electronic Signatures' (13 December 99). It was published in the Commission's *Official Journal* on 19 January 2000, Ref. L13/12. It can be found on: <http://www.europa.eu.int/comm/dg15/en>.

A useful Web page giving access to much of the material mentioned in this chapter is the European Commission's at: <http://bscw2.ispo.cec.be/ecommerce/Welcome.html>. Its 'Links' section is particularly useful.

The UK Electronic Communications Act is available at: <http://www.hmso.gov.uk>, under 'Legislation'.

A French draft bill on this area and its explanatory memorandum can be accessed at: <http://www.legifrance.gouv.fr>.

The DTI introductory guide for business, Home Shopping: New rights for consumers leaflet and FAQs for business are on the DTI Website at <http://www.dti.gov.uk/CACP/ca/dsdbulletin.htm>. A copy of the Regulations is also on the Website of the stationery office <www.hmso.gov.uk>. They are called The Consumer Protection (Distance Selling) Regulations 2000 (SI 2000/2334). A 1999 consultation on unsolicited goods laws is on the Internet at <http://www.dti.gov.uk/cacp/ca/goodserv.htm> DTI has published a detailed booklet *The consumer protection (distance selling) regulations 2000: A Guide for Business*, October 2000, see <www.dti.gov.uk>.

Information on EU electronic commerce legislation can be found at: <http://www.ispo.cec.be/ecommerce/legal.htm>.

EC REPORT ON DISTANCE SELLING AND COMPARATIVE ADVERTISING

On 10 March 2000, the European Commission prepared a 34-page report, *Consumer Complaints in Respect of Distance Selling and Comparative Advertising* (COM (2000) 127 final, 10 March 2000) which will be of interest for anyone following this area of law. Its purpose is to report on the results of studies and investigations carried out by the Commission on issues under the directives relating to complaints and remedies for consumers.

5 PROBLEMS

This chapter looks at what happens when things go wrong, disputes, defective goods and negotiations. It also provides advice on how to avoid things going wrong in the first place. Before any decision is made to sell goods or services over the Internet, the practical aspects must be fully considered. For example, if the supplier cannot be sure customers' banking transactions will be secure, it should not begin offering banking services online. If it does not have adequate distribution and warehousing facilities, its new Internet goods despatch service may end up a disaster. Those are technical, not legal matters, but legal contracts will underpin them, whether they be the contracts with the software company which licenses the security software, or the contract with the distribution company which ships the goods.

Here is a checklist for businesses selling goods or services over the Internet:

- Do we have written contracts with all those on whom we rely for software, Web services, despatch of goods, and so on?
- Do those contracts state clearly what happens if the contracts are breached? Do we have proper recourse?
- Are there clear acceptance tests or equivalent provisions in contracts with our own suppliers allowing us to check that software or other deliverables comply with the contract requirements, and which give us a right to reject the goods if they do not meet the contractual requirements?
- Is it clear which laws apply to the contracts?
- Does the contract say where disputes will be heard – in court, before an arbitrator, or only litigated once an alternative dispute-resolution procedure has been followed?
- Have we considered a 'guarantee' for customers which goes beyond that required by law, to give them confidence in trading over the Internet?

Insurance

Many businesses have legal expenses insurance. Software companies, for example, will often have professional indemnity insurance cover which protects them if they are sued for breach of contract or negligence arising from the software they have written for the customer. Often, the insurance company will want to check the clauses in the standard contract of such companies, to make sure they exclude liability to the fullest extent permitted by law. Some companies are therefore not allowed to alter their exclusion and limitation of liability clauses in their contracts without obtaining the prior written consent of the insurance company.

Other companies which supply goods or services over the Internet will have insurance cover against 'product liability' risks. This might, for example, include cover where the goods supplied physically harm the customer. Some such policies may exclude particular jurisdictions. Indeed, some UK suppliers exclude supplies of their products to certain countries where they do not have insurance. Check this before proceeding.

Always take legal advice on the exclusion and limitation of liability clauses in the contract. The law is full of traps. For example, if the clause excludes liability for death or personal injury, it will be void. So there is usually a clause saying this is not excluded. Someone without the requisite legal knowledge trying to shorten a clause or 'improve' it could easily render it wholly invalid by removing the exclusion from the clause for death and personal injury. The supplier has to accept liability for that risk.

Another mistake is to try to exclude all liability. In the UK, this is almost always void under the Unfair Contract Terms Act 1977 (or for contracts with consumers, the Unfair Terms in Consumer Contracts Regulations 1999). The careful lawyer will try to strike a balance between what it is reasonable to exclude, perhaps loss of profits or contracts, and what liability ought reasonably to be accepted. Meddle with such clauses only after taking legal advice and checking with the insurance company.

Notify insurers early when a dispute arises, otherwise the claim may not be covered. Do not wait for solicitors' letters or claims (formerly called 'writs') to arrive. Most policies require notification before then.

Security

Many consumers are put off using the Internet to purchase goods and services because of concerns that their credit card details may be disclosed. Ensure that a secure server is used. Where personal data is gathered, in the UK there is a legal duty under the Data Protection Act 1998 principles to keep data safe and secure. If a security breach occurs, bigger companies should speak to their public relations agencies to determine how best to address the matter.

From a legal point of view, the customer may be entitled to a refund and damages. Take legal advice. Those paying by credit card have protection, although there is legal doubt about the extent of that protection where they use a card for purchases abroad.

Contract negotiations

Many large contracts are despatched in draft form from supplier to buyer, or between their legal advisers, by e-mail. Indeed, in the author's firm at least 95 per cent of contract drafts are e-mailed between the parties with automatic highlighting of changes from draft to draft. Whether this is 'safe' or not is, in a sense, superseded by its being the standard practice. The advantage in saving time and making alterations quickly more than out-weigh any security risks. The old lawyer's 'travelling draft' with posted contracts and changes marked in different colours by hand on the draft is replaced by the much improved electronic version.

The obvious points to check are these:

- Have changes been made which are not highlighted? Always read the final draft before signature, in case the wrong version has been used or changes added without being spotted. In any event, this is sensible in case there are points no one had thought of until then.
- Do not write comments for only one side to read on the draft, as some word processing systems will allow the other party to restore and read them (for example, a note that 'We will see if we can get away with this clause, but will drop it if they object' may be seen!).
- Keep backup copies of drafts (lawyers often print them out and put them on the paper file for good backup and security reasons), because if a debate ensues about what was agreed when, or if the final contract wording is unclear, then the drafts become relevant.
- Check before starting the process that the other party is happy to e-mail draft contracts. Some companies have taken an informed decision not to send very secret commercial agreements by e-mail, and to do so would breach their own corporate policy. Solicitors, for example, will not use this means unless the client agrees and is happy with it.
- For some larger corporate deals, normally takeovers and mergers, law firms now set up Websites for that deal which are very secure.

- For very secret deals where one party is not happy with use of e-mail, consider using encryption technology. Remember that contracts sent by courier and fax also go astray from time to time.

Ambiguous terms

One of the worst requests from a client to their solicitor is to retain some wording in the contract which is ambiguous. The lawyer knows who will be blamed two years later when the contract comes under scrutiny and everyone has forgotten at whose request the ambiguity was retained. Also, even changing the contract to the other side's advantage is better than unclear wording. It is better to know where one stands than to have unclear wording.

In drafting contract terms, try to achieve the following:

- a clear definition section, and then use capital letters throughout the agreement for the defined terms
- lots of headings and sub-paragraphs
- short sentences
- avoid jargon – use clear English
- if a sentence is not understood, change it – do not assume the lawyers know what it means.

A bad example might be:

> The supplier undertakes and warrants to
> effect delivery of the software to the client.

The simple way to say the same thing would be: 'The supplier shall deliver the software to the client.'

Readers will be aware of much more extreme examples in practice. The aim of a written contract is to ensure certainty and clarity. Instead of a verbal, 'back of an envelope' arrangement, which is the norm in many industries where all sorts of important legal areas are left completely open, the parties know where they stand. They know what quality the product is to be. They know when it must be delivered. They know how much they can sue each other for if things go wrong.

The English laws of construction say that if wording is unclear, then it is construed against the person who drafted it. So make the contract clear.

However, be careful about making contracts shorter by removing terms. Most are there for a reason. The Internet makes it easier to have long conditions of contract, unlike with paper contracts, where the hardest task for the commercial solicitor is often ensuring that the terms and conditions of sale will fit on the back of the relevant order form and still be legible.

Clauses about disputes

The obvious clause about disputes in a contract will be headed 'choice of law and jurisdiction', and is likely to say that disputes go to court and that English law applies. It may say instead that disputes go to arbitration, which is a very similar process. Arbitration usually involves barristers and solicitors, and is usually not cheaper than going to court.

Mediation is something entirely different, which can be attempted first before court action/arbitration. Methods of alternative dispute-resolution are always worth trying (see below). Disputes are very expensive when they go to court or arbitration, particularly if they relate to intellectual property rights, disputes over which country's laws apply, or complex contractual matters. All three of these features are common in Internet disputes. The *Godfrey* v. *Demon* libel case (see page 7), for example, reportedly led to legal costs of over £250,000. This is not at all unusual. If there is an insurance company paying the costs, that is a different matter, but they too will take control of the action, and may well settle it early.

Waiver

Another clause relevant in this area is called the 'waiver' – this says that if a breach of contract happens but one side does nothing about it, they can later complain. In other words, any waiving of the breach or acquiescence will not be held against them later. If that clause is not there, then a failure to act at once on a breach of contract could lead to the rights being lost. However, whether there is a waiver clause or not, it is wise at least to write to the other party complaining of the breach, for the record.

Alternative dispute-resolution

Before going either to court or arbitration with a dispute, alternative methods of resolution can be tried if both parties are willing. Neither will be held to any decision reached, unlike before a judge or arbitrator who decides the case, but if agreement is reached, then the mediation can result in both parties signing a 'settlement' agreement which is then legally binding.

THE CENTRE FOR DISPUTE RESOLUTION

There are number of mediation bodies in the UK. The Centre for Dispute Resolution is one of the best-known. The 'further information' section at the end of this chapter gives a list of alternative dispute-resolution bodies.

COMMUNITY LEGAL SERVICE

A useful source of advice for legal disputes is the Website <http://www.justask.org.uk>, which provides links to bodies such as the Law Society and Citizens' Advice Bureaux.

SOCIETY OF COMPUTERS AND LAW

The Society of Computers and Law is a useful body to join for those with an interest in Internet law in the UK: <http://www.scl.org>.

Some contracts provide in their dispute-resolution clause that the expert will sit as an expert, and not an arbitrator, to determine a particular factual/technical matter in dispute. It can be useful to approach a body such as the Society of Computers and Law for names of possible experts whom the parties could use.

Going to court

Before going to court, always try to settle a dispute. As a practising solicitor who regularly handles computer litigation, the author always tells clients it will cost twice whatever they are quoted, and take twice as long. Rarely does anyone involved in litigation or arbitration revel in the process. Frequently, they wish they had never started it. The difficulty is that it is not known at the start whether issuing the court claim will be the end of the matter or the start of over two or three years of regular, often daily, contact with solicitors. It is not just the legal costs which must be considered, but the diverting of management time. It is not surprising that over 90 per cent of cases which even get as far as court proceedings being issued (and those cases going that far are themselves rare) are settled before a trial. The English court process and the Civil Procedure Rules are designed to keep people out of court. Alternative dispute-resolution is now strongly recommended, and the judge will ask whether the parties have tried it.

If a case is going to court, it is generally advisable to use solicitors for English legal disputes. In practice, the aim will be to head off matters before they get to this stage. Be careful about the following:

- Do not admit liability. This might negate any insurance policy, and may also mean that the case will be lost if it is subsequently litigated.
- Do say 'We are sorry you are unhappy with our service' or some other apology which does not involve an admission. Take legal advice on the precise wording.
- If trying to settle a dispute, mark letters 'Without prejudice' (this means they are clearly an attempt to settle a dispute and will not be seen by a court later – they are kept 'off the record').
- Before agreement is reached, mark letters 'Subject to contract', to make it clear that any offers are still in the preliminary stages.
- Pick up on small breaches of contract early on, so that large problems do not accumulate. Do not be afraid of pointing out problems. It can be done in a tactful way.
- If a dispute under foreign laws arises, go to lawyers in the correct jurisdiction.
- Keep all letters. Keep file notes of meetings. Documents often win a case later.
- Use psychology as much as law. Often, two aggressive businesspeople will dig their heels in over a dispute entirely unnecessarily. Never litigate on principle. Always be prepared to pay a small sum even if entirely in the right, just to be rid of a legal dispute which might cost thousands in costs, no matter how galling that might seem.
- Seek advice from trade associations, which often have valuable experience.
- Threatening letters can lead to legal liability. Take advice before writing them.
- Do not air the dispute in public. Courts hate that, it could lead to libel actions, and will just put off both parties' customers. Settle quickly and secretly.
- Any settlement must be drawn up carefully by lawyers, to ensure it is effective and in full and final settlement of all claims.

Further information

CONTACTS

For disputes about domain names, see Chapter 3, and in particular the systems run by ICANN and WIPO: <http://www.icann.org> and <http://www.wipo.org>.

The Community Legal Service
<http://www.justask.org.uk>

The Society of Computers and Law
Ms Caroline Gould, SCL Headquarters, 10 Hurle Crescent, Clifton, Bristol, BS8 2TA. tel.: (+44) (0)117 923 7393. fax: (+44) (0)117 923 9305. e-mail: <caroline.gould@scl.org>. Website: <http://www.scl.org>

DISPUTE-RESOLUTION BODIES

Academy of Experts
2 South Square, Gray's Inn, London WC1R 5HP. tel.: (+44) (0)20 7637 0333. fax: (+44) (0)20 7637 1893. e-mail: <Admin@academy-experts.org>. Website: <http://www.academy-experts.org>

ADR Group
Grove House, Grove Road, Redland, Bristol BS6 6UN. tel.: (+44) (0)117 946 7180. fax: (+44) (0)117 946 7181. e-mail: <info@adrgroup.co.uk>. Website: <http://www.adrgroup.co.uk>

Centre for Dispute Resolution
Princes House, 95 Gresham Street, London, EC2V 7NA. tel.: (+44) (0)20 7600 0500. fax: (+44) (0)20 7600 0501. e-mail: <mediate@cedr.co.uk>. Website: <http://www.cedr.co.uk>

The Chartered Institute of Arbitrators
24 Angel Gate, City Road, London EC1V 2RS. tel.: (+44) (0)20 7837 4483. fax: (+44) (0)20 7837 4185. e-mail: <info@arbitrators.org>. Website: <http://www.arbitrators.org>

City Disputes Panel
Fifth Floor, 3 London Wall Buildings, London EC2M 5PD. tel.: (+44)
(0)20 7638 4775. fax: (+44) (0)20 7638 4776. e-mail:
<CDPlondon@aol.com>. Website <http://members.aol.com/cdplondon/
cdp.html>

Mediation UK
Alexander House, Telephone Avenue, Bristol BS1 4BS. tel.: (+44) (0)117
904 6661. fax: (+44) (0)117 904 3331. e-mail:
<mediationuk@mediationuk.org.uk>. Website: <http://
www.mediationuk.org.uk>

APPENDICES

APPENDIX 1 COMPUTER USE POLICY

We do not wish to restrict in any way your full use of our computer system, either on a personal basis or in your work for us – indeed, we encourage it. However, we regard the integrity of our computer system as key to the success of our business. Our Computer Security Officer is ____, to whom you should direct any queries about this policy. To avoid misunderstanding and confusion, all employees must abide by the following policies.

1   Licensed software

Only correctly licensed software may be loaded onto our computers. You are not allowed to use within the Company any material that you either know, or suspect to be, in breach of copyright. In addition, you are not allowed to pass such material on to anyone else. It is important to bear in mind that breach of copyright for business purposes can be a criminal offence, both by the Company *and* the individual concerned. No software may be loaded without first obtaining the express permission of the Computer Security Officer. Software includes business applications, shareware, entertainment software, games, screensavers and demonstration software. If you are unsure whether a piece of software requires a licence, please contact the Computer Security Officer. The copying of software media and manuals is also prohibited.

2   Networks

None of our PCs may be connected to a customer network without permission from both the Computer Security Officer and written permission from the customer concerned. In addition, none of our PCs may be connected to a public network, for example, the Internet, without permission from the Computer Security Officer.

3 Disks

You must not use disks from unknown sources or from home computers. All data disks must be virus-checked before they may be used on our computer system.

4 Viruses

More damage to files is generally caused by inappropriate corrective action than by the viruses themselves. If a virus is suspected, you must turn the computer off and leave it off until you find out what to do. The matter should be reported immediately to the Computer Security Officer.

5 Customer procedures

You must observe the customer's rules relating to computers if you work at a customer's premises. In the absence of such rules, our rules should be followed.

6 Access

You are only permitted access to those parts of our computer system which you need in order to carry out your normal duties.

7 Inappropriate material

You are not allowed to view or download any pornographic material on our computer system, or place obscene or offensive screensavers on your PC.

8 Data protection

If you have access to personal data, you are in a particularly sensitive position and must bear in mind at all times the provisions of the Data Protection Act 1998. Guidance on these may be obtained from the Computer Security Officer.

9   Passwords

You must use passwords at all times, and change them at the intervals notified to you. You must not select obvious passwords. All passwords must be kept confidential.

10   Backups

Regular backups must be carried out in accordance with the rules laid down from time to time.

11   E-mail and Internet use policy

In line with the normal rules that apply to you as an employee, you are not allowed to send racist, defamatory, obscene, indecent or abusive messages on our computer system, either internally or externally. Any use by you of e-mail or the Internet shall be governed by our 'E-mail and Internet Use Policy', which shall be notified to you separately.

12   Misuse

Misuse of computers is a serious disciplinary offence. The following are examples of misuse:

(a) fraud and theft
(b) system sabotage
(c) introduction of viruses and time bombs
(d) using unauthorized software
(e) obtaining unauthorized access
(f) using the system for unauthorized private work or game-playing
(g) breaches of the Data Protection Act 1998
(h) sending abusive, rude or defamatory messages via electronic mail
(i) hacking
(j) breach of company security procedures.

This list is not exhaustive. Depending on the circumstances of each case, misuse of the computer system is likely to be considered gross misconduct, punishable by dismissal without notice. Misuse amounting to criminal conduct may be reported by us to the Police.

13 Breaches

We have the right by law to monitor anything that is on our computer system (both personal and business). However, we do not intend to do so unless we have reasonable grounds for believing that a problem has arisen. All breaches of computer security must be referred to the Computer Security Officer. If you suspect that a fellow employee (of whatever seniority) is abusing the computer system, you may speak in confidence to the Personnel Department. You are responsible for any actions that are taken against us by a third party arising from restricted and/or offensive material being displayed or sent by you on our computer system.

14 Improvements

We welcome suggestions from you for the improvement of this policy.

© Clark Holt 2000. These terms and conditions were drafted by Clark Holt, Commercial Solicitors, who specialize exclusively in commercial law, with a particular emphasis on the Internet.

Clark Holt, 1 Sanford Street, Swindon, Wiltshire SN1 1QQ, tel. (+44) (0)1793 617444, fax (+44) (0)1793 617436, Website <http://www.clarkholt.co.uk>

APPENDIX 2   E-MAIL AND INTERNET USE POLICIES

There follow two examples of e-mail and Internet policies with slightly different emphases. You should feel free to adapt and combine these as best suits your circumstances, taking legal advice where appropriate.

Policy A

1   INTRODUCTION: USE OF E-MAIL

1.1   We encourage employees to use e-mail at work. It saves time and expense. However, we do require that you follow the simple rules below. These are part of your staff handbook, with which, in turn, you are required to comply under your employment contract. A serious breach of these rules could lead to dismissal. If you are unsure about whether anything you propose to do might breach our e-mail policy, speak to your manager or the Company Secretary for advice first.

1.2   Although we encourage the use of e-mail, it can be risky. You need to be careful not to introduce viruses on to our system. You need to take proper account of the security advice below. You must make sure you do not send libellous statements in e-mails, as the company could be liable for damages.

1.3   These rules are designed to minimize the legal risks we run when you use e-mail at work and access the Internet. They are also designed to tell you what you may and may not do at work in this area. If there is something we have not covered and you do not know what our policy is, then ask your manager or the Company Secretary. Do not assume you know the right answer.

1.4   Technology and the law change all the time, and this policy will be updated regularly. It is your responsibility to read the latest version of this document, which will be both e-mailed and sent to you in the internal mail.

2   USING THE INTERNET AT WORK

2.1   **Authorized Internet users**: If you have been provided with a computer with Internet access at your desk, you may use the Internet at work. If there is access through one terminal in your department and you have been told you may use the Internet, then again you may do so. If you have not been told or do not know, then ask.

2.2   Not everyone in the Company needs access to the Internet at work. If you think you do, but have not been given access so far, then contact your manager and make a written request, setting out the reasons why you think the access should be allowed.

2.3   You are not allowed to arrange your own Internet access on the PC on your desk. All Internet access must be officially sanctioned and put in place by our trained IT professionals.

2.4   **Personal laptops**: You may not bring your own laptop or palmtop or other computer into work to surf the Internet during working hours unless you have been permitted to do so by your manager. The reason for this is that use of the Internet where the Company does not deem it necessary can waste time in your working day for the Company. Also, we cannot monitor the access you make over your own system in the way we can over our own systems.

2.5   If you are allowed access to the Internet at work, then you are expected to use it sensibly and not so that it interferes with efficient working for the Company. For example, if it would be quicker for you to call a standards body than do a long-winded Internet search, then make a telephone call instead. You may be called upon to justify the amount of time you have spent on the Internet or the sites you have visited, so always bear this in mind when surfing the net.

2.6   We encourage those to whom we give Internet access to become familiar with the Internet, and do not currently impose any time limitation on work-related Internet use. We trust employees not to abuse the latitude we give them, but if this trust is abused, then we reserve the right to alter the policy in this respect.

2.7 **Removing Internet access**: We can at any time deny Internet access to any employee at work without giving any reason, although normally we would provide reasons.

2.8 **Registering on Websites**: If you want to register as a user of a Website for work purposes, this is encouraged. Many such sites are very useful for the Company, and a large number require a registration. You should ask your manager in advance, however, so we are sure of that to which you may be committing the Company, and to ensure the registration will not result in our being inundated with junk mail.

2.9 **Licences and contracts**: Some sites through which you can access free work-related information and documents will require the Company to enter into licence or contract terms. These terms would be checked by our legal department in the normal way. The fact they are electronic does not affect our normal rules in this respect. Print out the terms and send them for approval in advance, or e-mail them to the legal department before you agree to them on the Company's behalf. In most cases they will be unobjectionable, and the free information to which you will then be entitled may save the Company money. However, always consider whether the information is from a reputable source and is likely to be accurate and kept up to date. Most of the contract terms you will be required to sign up to will exclude liability for accuracy for such free information.

2.10 **Downloading files and software**: Only download files onto PCs with virus-checking software, and check how long the download will take. If you are uncertain as to whether the time it will take is reasonable, ask your line manager. In some cases it will be cheaper for us to order the software or file on disk by telephone rather than spending, for example, two hours downloading a file which may prevent your doing your normal work in the mean time. Check with our IT department before you download software. It may not be compatible with our system, or may cause other problems.

2.11 **Using other software at work**: Our staff handbook does not allow you to bring software into the office from home without the IT department's consent, and nothing in this 'E-mail and Internet Policy' modifies our general policies on such software use.

3   USING THE INTERNET FOR PERSONAL PURPOSES

3.1 Where you are given access to the Internet at work, you may access the Internet for personal purposes, using our systems, during your official lunch and rest breaks, but at no other times, provided no other employee needs use of the PC for work-related purposes, as long as:

- such use is limited to no more than 20 minutes in any day,
- you do not order goods or services, including stocks and shares, without your manager's permission (in many cases this may be granted, but we want to know about this in advance),
- you do not access any site which will result in charges being levied for such access over and above the cost of the local call in most Internet access,
- you do not use the Internet to access unlawful material – if by accident you access unlawful material, you should send an e-mail to your manager so we know the circumstances (the access may be picked up by our monitoring system); (for these purposes, unlawful material is that which breaks English law, such as child pornography, and also searches within the law but which may expose the Company to liability for sexual harassment by other colleagues who may see what you are searching – such as soft pornography),
- you do not enter into any contracts or commitments in the name of or on behalf of the Company,
- you do not arrange for any goods ordered after you have obtained your manager's approval to be delivered to our address, or order them in the Company's name.

3.2 You are not allowed to use the Internet at other times for personal purposes, including before working hours begin or after they end. We have security concerns about staff arriving early and leaving late, and it is harder for us to monitor your use of the Internet at such times. During your working hours, you must not surf the Internet at all for personal purposes. This is in line with our policy on the use of office telephones and faxes and our restriction on your use of your personal mobile telephone to official breaks only. If you are not sure what a 'personal purpose' is, ask your manager. It means something unrelated to your job.

4 USE OF E-MAIL

4.1 Where we have given you access to e-mail at work, you may send work-related e-mails.

4.2 Staff may not send or receive personal e-mails at work using the Company's computers. Staff using their own laptop or palmtops or personal organizers to send private e-mails shall do so only in official lunch and rest breaks, and not use the Company name or affiliations in any way.

4.3 Ensure our official corporate information is given on the e-mail, as notified to you. This is set out below, but may be varied from time to time. You will be given notice of variations.

```
John Smith
IT Manager
ABC plc
Company No. 123456789
123 Big Road, Bigtown, Big County AB1 1BA, UK
Tel (+44) (1)11 1111 111
Fax (+44) (1)11 1111 111

The contents of this e-mail may be confidential and are protected by copyright. If you
receive it in error, call us on the number above and do not use, retain or copy it.
```

4.4 Read e-mails carefully several times before sending them. It is just as important as with a letter that they are accurate and do not contain typing and spelling errors. They are often the written public face of the Company. In many cases, for longer e-mails it may be better to prepare the message offline and check it carefully before despatch.

4.5 **Libel**: The Company can be sued for libel if you make inaccurate statements in your e-mails which disparage or denigrate other people or companies. This could lead to our having to pay hundreds of thousands of pounds in damages, and you would lose your job. Therefore, read all messages carefully before sending them, and if in doubt at all about what you have written, check the content with your manager first.

4.6 **CC-ing**: Be very careful not to copy e-mails automatically to all those sent copies of the original message to which you are replying. It is easy to do this, and can mean a message is seen by someone you do not want to see it. It may mean you disclose confidential company information to the wrong person. Disable the automatic 'cc-ing back' function on the e-mail program, and then with each e-mail consider who should be sent a copy of it.

4.7 Statements to avoid include criticizing our competitors or their staff, stating there are quality problems with goods or services of suppliers or customers, and stating anyone is incompetent.

4.8 If you prepare an e-mail and your overall feeling is that you are glad you have 'got it off your chest', it is probably a signal it should not be sent. Do not prepare such e-mails. It is easy for you or your secretary to send them in error, or for them to be seen by someone else. It rarely reflects well on the Company, in any event, to criticize others. The quality of our goods and services speaks for itself.

4.9   Do not attach anything to an e-mail which may contain a virus. The Company could be liable to the recipient for loss suffered. We have virus-checking in place, but check with our IT department in cases of doubt. Be very careful about forwarding attachments from third parties, particularly unidentified third parties. These may carry viruses, and they may also not have been cleared for copyright issues. You may breach copyright by sending them on to someone else, as you are making a further copy. The Company could be sued for large damages for breach of copyright.

4.10   **E-mail Monitoring**: We routinely monitor your e-mails and Websites accessed at work to ensure compliance with the law, in the same way your manager may read your business letters and faxes. If you want to send confidential non-work-related e-mails, do so on your own equipment in your own time at your own home.

5   CONTRACTS

5.1   You should have been told by the Company whether you have authority to enter into contracts on behalf of the Company. If you do not know, ask your manager. You may be subject to a financial limit above which you may not enter into contracts. Stick to these rules and limits when ordering goods or services or supplying them via e-mail. Most staff are not allowed to make contracts on the Company's behalf. However, what follows below will apply to our procurement/buying department and our contracts department.

5.2   The Company is happy for contracts to be formed electronically, and encourages this to be done. However, it should only be done by those with authority, should accord with our contract management policy in any event, and should follow the rules below for electronic contracts:

- Do not order anything without knowing the delivery dates and whether they are legally binding; the price; clear description of the goods; full identity of the supplier; payment method, and delivery charges if any. Be cautious about ordering high-value goods or services with payment in advance.
- Read the terms and conditions, and print out a copy for the relevant paper file. We may need to refer to the terms later if a legal dispute arises. Make sure you are happy with them. Check them with our legal department.

- Try to enter contracts on our own terms and conditions of purchase wherever possible, in the usual way. Our lawyers can advise you on how to do this.
- Conversely, when you agree on behalf of the Company to supply goods or services, make sure you use our standard terms and conditions of supply.
- The contract terms should be sent before the contract is made, otherwise it may be too late in contract law terms for them to form part of the legal arrangement. This is very important.
- Make sure you have a supplier telephone number, fax and physical address and full company name, otherwise we may have no practical recourse against the supplier if things go wrong.
- Ensure you know when a contract is made – when we are legally bound to proceed. Do not pull out or attempt to pull out after that stage without taking legal advice first.

5.3   Where there is a negotiated contract, take advice from our Company Secretary or legal department about whether in that case we are happy to send contract drafts by e-mail. In many cases we are, but some deals are particularly secret and other methods must be used. If we are happy with this, then do be careful to check for changes made by the other company. Sometimes a marked-up draft does not show all the changes. Also, watch out for disclosure of any comments you make on the draft. Although you may think you have deleted them before sending them to the other company, they may be readable using some word processing software.

5.4   When you reach the final contract signature stage, at present we still require a physical signature on negotiated contracts of this type, so ensure a faxed or posted or couriered copy of the contract is signed. New laws being adopted at present may lead to recognition of 'digital signatures', so this may change in due course, and we will advise you of this.

6   COPYRIGHT

6.1   Most information available electronically is protected by copyright in the same way as a book, music or a play is. The Copyright, Designs and Patents Act 1988 sets out the rules, and you must be careful not to breach copyright. If you do, then the Company could have to pay thousands of pounds in damages, and you could lose your job.

6.2   It is easy to copy electronically, but this does not make it any less an offence. The Company's policy is to comply with copyright laws. We do not bend the rules in any way. We do not allow the use of pirated or copied computer software. All software must be licensed. We take this very seriously indeed, and have regular audits to check the position. We have a separate Company policy on use of software at work, which also applies. Nothing in this document alters that policy.

6.3 Do not assume that because a document or file is on the Internet or our intranet, for example, that it can be freely copied. There is a difference between information in the 'public domain' (which is certainly then no longer confidential or secret information, but is still copyright-protected) and information which is not protected by copyright (such as where the author has been dead for more than 70 years under the 1988 Act).

6.4 Copyright and database right law can be complicated. Speak to your manager or the legal department/Company Secretary if you are unsure about anything.

6.5 Lots of information on the Internet says what its copyright conditions are, so read those before downloading or copying. For example, the Department of Trade and Industry produces useful guidance notes on many areas relevant to our business. We would encourage those of you with Internet access to download these, but you would not be permitted to reproduce them in a book or other Company document without obtaining separate consent.

6.6 Nor must you circulate newspaper cuttings, even if just about the Company, without speaking to the Company Secretary first. We do pay for an annual licence from the Newspaper Licensing Agency, but you must check first what this covers.

6.7 If someone tells you to ignore these rules, even your manager, do not listen to them. Report the matter to our Company Secretary or a director.

7   TRADE MARKS, LINKS AND DATA PROTECTION

7.1 The Company's name is a registered trade mark. If you come across anyone using the same or a similar name, let your manager know. We may need to stop them doing this. But do not send any threatening e-mails to them about this, as that could be an offence under the Trade Marks Act 1994. Our lawyers will handle that side of things.

7.2 You must not register any new domain names or trade marks relating to the Company's names or products anywhere in the world, unless the Company has authorized it. Nor should you link any of our Web pages to any others without checking first with your manager and the Company Secretary.

7.3 If you see anything on our Website which is not up to date, let your manager know, as for legal and public relations reasons we need to keep it accurate and current.

7.4 The Company is registered under the Data Protection Act 1998. The 8th Data Protection Principle restricts those countries to which we can send 'personal data', whether by e-mail or any other means. 'Personal data' would be information such as names and addresses or other personal details. Certain data, such as about people's race or religion, is called 'sensitive personal data', and is subject to even stricter rules. You must take legal advice before exporting data. For example, even sending a candidate's curriculum vitae from the personnel office in the UK to our associated companies outside the EU could breach the rules if we do not take special measures.

8 GENERAL

8.1 The aim of these rules is to be helpful. They are not aimed at putting employees off using the Internet or e-mail. We encourage the use of the Internet and e-mail. It is a major opportunity for our business.

8.2 If there is anything in the rules which becomes unworkable or which you do not understand, let your manager know and we will do our best to correct or alter the rules. We want them to work and be understood. If you notice another employee not following the code, tell them and your manager.

8.3 No matter what we say in these rules or in any other Company document, your overriding objective must be to obey the law. The Company will never ask you to breach the law, whatever the circumstances. Contact a director or our external legal advisers if you think you have been asked to do so.

8.4 We sometimes use self-employed contractors or individuals employed by agencies in our Company. They will have signed our standard contractor's agreement. They should also be subject to the rules set out in this document, where applicable. If you are working with such contractors, show them the rules. The same applies to new members of staff, who ought to be shown a copy.

Signed: Managing Director, the Company
Version 1. 1 May 2001

Policy B

We do not wish to restrict in any way your full use of e-mail or access to the Internet in your work for us – indeed, we encourage it. However, we regard the integrity of our computer system as key to the success of our business. Our Computer Security Officer is ____, to whom you should direct any queries about this policy. To avoid misunderstanding and confusion, all employees must abide by the following policies.

1 USE OF THE INTERNET AT WORK

The primary reason for our providing you with access to the Internet and/or e-mail is to assist you in your work for us. You are allowed to send personal e-mails and to go on to the Internet, provided that such activities do not affect your ability to work properly for us during normal working hours.

2 ORDERS

You are not allowed to order anything on our behalf by e-mail without proper authorization. You should always bear in mind that an e-mail from the Company has the same legal effect as a letter from the Company on the Company's notepaper. This underlines the importance of being careful with what you say in an e-mail, in case it is misunderstood.

All e-mails must contain our standard footer, which will be notified to you from time to time.

3 CONFIDENTIALITY

Before sending any confidential information by e-mail, you should consider carefully whether appropriate steps have been taken to maintain such confidentiality. Electronic mail is not inherently a more secure medium of communication than traditional means, and can be easily copied, forwarded and archived.

4 VIRUSES

The most likely way that our computer system will be infected by a virus will be by an external message. Any outside material must be properly virus-checked before being loaded onto our computer system.

5   INAPPROPRIATE MATERIAL

In line with the normal rules that apply to you as an employee, you are not allowed to send racist, defamatory, obscene, indecent or abusive messages on our computer system, either internally or externally. Do be careful and think carefully before sending any questionable messages that could reflect badly on us as a Company. You are not allowed to view or download any pornographic material on our computer system or place obscene or offensive screensavers on your PC.

6   SECURITY

You must not give internal passwords to anyone outside the Company. In addition, you must not give any customer-related security information to anyone other than the customer unless specifically authorized in writing by the customer in advance.

When dealing with any personal data, you should always bear in mind the rules relating to data protection that apply to such data.

7   LICENSED SOFTWARE

The only software that may be used on our computer system is software that has been properly licensed to us. You are not allowed to use within the Company any software that you either know, or suspect to be, in breach of copyright. In addition, you are not allowed to pass such material on to anyone else. It is important to bear in mind that any breach of copyright for business purposes can be a criminal offence, both by the Company and the individual concerned.

8   RECORDS

You are expected to keep proper records of our dealings with outsiders. It is always possible that what appears to be a relatively trivial point could be of immense significance later. It is not possible to foresee what will subsequently need to be checked.

9   USE OF OUR COMPUTER SYSTEM

Any use by you of our computer system shall be governed by our 'Computer Use Policy', which shall be notified to you separately.

10   BREACHES

We have the right by law to monitor anything (including e-mails) that is on our computer system (both personal and business). However, we do not intend to do so unless we have reasonable grounds for believing that a problem has arisen. All breaches of computer security must be referred to the Computer Security Officer. If you suspect that a fellow employee (of whatever seniority) is abusing the computer system, you may speak in confidence to the personnel department. You are responsible for any actions that are taken against us by a third party arising from restricted and/or offensive material being displayed or sent by you on our computer system. Depending on the circumstances in each case, breach of this policy by you could amount to gross misconduct punishable by dismissal without notice. Misuse amounting to criminal conduct may be reported by us to the Police.

11   IMPROVEMENTS

We welcome suggestions from you for the improvement of this policy.

© Clark Holt 2000. These terms and conditions were drafted by Clark Holt, Commercial Solicitors, who specialize exclusively in commercial law, with a particular emphasis on the Internet.

Clark Holt, 1 Sanford Street, Swindon, Wiltshire SN1 1QQ,
tel. (+44) (0)1793 617444, fax (+44) (0)1793 617436,
Website <http://www.clarkholt.co.uk>.

APPENDIX 3   INTERNET TERMS AND CONDITIONS

The legal issues relevant to what legal conditions and notices should be placed on a Website are similar to those applying to general terms and conditions of sale or purchase, which, like Website conditions, are never signed. The important issue is to draw them to the attention of the user of the site. It is even better if the user has to click to indicate acceptance, which may be possible where a user completes an online form for use of a more substantial site than one which is simply a glorified sales brochure.

Terms and conditions for use of a Website appear below, but simply as an example. No two cases are the same, and there are many others to examine on the Internet. Never just copy a set. Apart from breaching copyright, the terms will not all be appropriate anyway. They will always need some customization.

Copyright and trade mark notices

COPYRIGHT

It is wise to include a notice saying that the information on the site is protected by copyright, as shown below.

© EFG Limited 2001
All Rights Reserved

- The material on this site is protected by copyright and/or database right throughout the world, and is owned by EFG Limited or its licensors.
- You may read, print and download it for private use.
- You may not commercialize or otherwise copy it without our permission.
- Use of this Site is subject to our Terms and Conditions [LINK].

TRADE MARKS

Where the trade marks are registered, the symbol ® is used. ™ is only used for unregistered marks:

'EFG'™ and 'ABC'™ are trade names of EFG.

If third parties' trade marks are used, it may be necessary to include their notices too. Never use a mark without considering whether consent is needed.

FURTHER INFORMATION

For copyright and trade mark enquiries, contact:
The Copyright Manager, EFG Limited, ____.
Telephone: (+44) (0) ____. Facsimile: (+44) (0) ____.
E-mail: <copyright@efg.co.uk>.

Privacy policy

Most reputable Websites have a privacy policy on the site. It is essential to take legal advice on the Data Protection Act 1998 and its application to the site and the personal data gleaned therefrom.

There is advice about the Internet and data protection on the Website of the UK Information Commissioner, who is in charge of the legislation in this area. This is available at: <http://www.dataprotection.gov.uk>.

An example of a privacy policy is given below. However, the important question is what will be done with the data. Data must only be used where the data subject (individual) has consented to the use, and they must also be told the purposes for which the data will be held. All this information should appear in the policy. If the data will be exported, for example, then consent in the conditions may be needed from the data subject. If the data is 'sensitive' data as defined in the Act, explicit consent is needed for its further use.

Under the Act, the data controller must notify (register). This can be done online at: <http://www.dpr.gov.uk>.

PRIVACY POLICY

EFG's commitment to privacy

EFG Limited is committed to protecting the privacy of those using our site and the confidentiality of the personal information with which our subscribers provide us.

Data Protection Act 1998

We are registered under the Data Protection Act 1998, and comply with the Act in all our dealings with your personal data.

Your personal information is safe with us

EFG will never sell personal information or share personal information with third parties unrelated to it. At EFG, we use the information we collect to serve our customers in the following ways:

- If you become a subscriber to EFG or a user of other EFG services, your name, e-mail address, postal address and other information on the subscription form are kept by us and used to remind you when your next subscription is due and to send you the *EFG Report*.
- We may also use your contact information to let you know about enhancements to the site and your subscription entitlements. If you would rather not receive this information, please inform us by e-mail at: <privacy@efg.co.uk>.
- We do not use *cookies* (defined below) for collecting user information from the site, and we will not collect any information about you except that required for system administration of the Web server.

Cookies

A cookie is a message given to a *Web browser* by a *Web server*. The message is then stored by the browser. Each time the browser requests a page from the server, this message is sent back. A cookie's main objective is to identify users and personalize their visit by customizing web pages for them, for example by welcoming them by name next time they visit the same site. A site using cookies will usually invite you to provide personal information, such as your name, e-mail address and interests.

Further information

For further information on data protection and privacy, contact:
The Data Protection Manager, EFG Limited, ____.
Telephone: (+44) (0) ____. Facsimile (+44) (0) ____.
E-mail <privacy@efg.co.uk>.

Information on the Data Protection Act 1998 is also on the UK Information Commissioner's Website at: <http://www.dataprotection.gov.uk>.

Use of this Site is subject to our Terms and Conditions [LINK].

Children's Online Privacy Protection Act 1998

The USA has strict laws (COPPA) which came into force on 21 April 2000 governing personal data gathered from children under 13. It has been estimated that compliance with these laws costs the average UK Website aimed at children about US$50,000.

UK companies involved with children should check whether the US laws may apply to them. If so, information on the site will need to be drafted accordingly. The US legislation can be downloaded in pdf format at: <http://www.ftc.gov/os/1999/9910/64fr59888.pdf>. It is 29 pages long. Further information on the new US legislation is available at <http://www.ftc.gov/opa/1999/9910/childfinal.htm>, where the full text of the US legislation can also be accessed.

Corporate information

The dubious sites on the Internet avoid showing their name and address. The reputable sites give large amounts of corporate information. Companies should therefore be encouraged to provide adequate disclosure. For public companies, the annual report and accounts can appear. Charts of the corporate structure are useful, as are details of offices around the world. Before putting employees' personal data, photographs, and so on on the Internet, obtain their consent in order to ensure compliance with the Data Protection Act 1998.

Sample wording about a fictional company appears below.

ABOUT EFG LIMITED

EFG Limited is a private limited company incorporated in England, Company Number ____.

Its registered office is at ____.

EFG's business/correspondence address is ____. Telephone: (+44) (0) ____.
Facsimile: (+44) (0) ____. E-mail: <____>.

Terms and conditions for a Website

The conditions below are simply an example. Many sites differ substantially. The example below is for a site where contributors/surfers submit information to be used on the site, hence some of the specific provisions, particularly relating to copyright, would not always be necessary.

TERMS AND CONDITIONS FOR USE OF WEBSITE <http:// www.the-efg.com> AND CONTRIBUTIONS TO BULLETIN BOARDS

These are the terms and conditions of EFG Limited of ____. Telephone: (+44) (0) ____. Facsimile: (+44) (0) ____. E-mail: <____>.

1 Use of Website on these conditions

All use of the Website <www.the-efg.com> ('the Website') is on the terms and conditions below.

If you do not agree to these conditions, cease use of the Website immediately.

You may print and keep a copy of these terms. They are a legal agreement between us and can only be modified with our consent. We reserve the right to change the terms at our discretion by changing them on the Website.

Where goods or services are purchased on the Website (when available in due course), these are on our Terms and Conditions of Supply, not these terms.

2 Accuracy of information

EFG ('we') do our best to ensure all information on the Website is accurate.

If you find any inaccurate information on the Website let us know and we will correct it, where we agree, as soon as practicable.

You should ensure information you send to us is accurate and does not breach anyone else's rights, such as copyright, nor is libellous, obscene, menacing, threatening, offensive, abusive, fraudulent, criminal or infringes the rights of other people, nor is in any way illegal. Remember that the Website can be viewed around the world and the information you send to us will be published on the Website.

You should verify any information independently before relying upon it.

We make no representations that information is accurate and up to date or complete, and accept no liability for any loss or damage caused by inaccurate information. This Website gives a large amount of statistical data, and there will inevitably be errors in it.

3 Copyright and contributions to the site

You must make sure that you own all the intellectual property rights, including copyright and database right, in contributions which you send to us to publish on the Website ('Contributions'), or that you have permission from the rights owner to do this and that no contract, confidentiality or other obligation would prevent your making the Contribution.

You must identify who the rights holder is, and send to us your and their address and name as well as e-mail address when making a Contribution, in case we have any queries.

Anonymous Contributions are not accepted.

You should retain copies of all Contributions and other postings and information you send to us electronically, through the Website or otherwise.

You waive your moral rights to be identified as author of the Contribution and let us modify the Contribution. It may, for example, be necessary to shorten Contributions or cut them to fit the Website.

If there are any restrictions on the use to which we can put the Contribution, we must be told in advance, and we may have to reject it. We reserve the right to reject any Contribution at our discretion.

All Contributions received will be assumed to be for publication on the Website and any further use, at its discretion, of EFG on an exclusive, royalty-free perpetual basis. Where Contributions are written specifically for the Website, copyright and other intellectual property rights shall on their creation vest in EFG Ltd.

The Website contains copyright material, trade names and other proprietary information, including, but not limited to, text, software, photos and graphics, and may in future include video, graphics, music and sound. The entire contents of the Website are protected by copyright law. We, or our licensors, own copyright and/or database right in the selection, co-ordination, arrangement and enhancement of such content, as well as in the content original to it. You may not modify, publish, transmit, participate in the transfer or sale, create derivative works, or in any way exploit any of the content, in whole or in part, except as provided in these Terms.

You may download information from the Website for your own personal use only. Except as otherwise expressly permitted under copyright law, no copying, redistribution, retransmission, publication or commercial exploitation of downloaded material will be permitted without our express permission and that of the copyright owner. In the event of any permitted copying, redistribution or publication of copyright material, no changes in or deletion of author attribution, trademark legend or copyright notice shall be made. You acknowledge that you do not acquire any ownership rights by downloading copyright material.

EFG™ and ABC™ and our logos on this site are trade names of EFG Limited. You may not use those names without our consent.

4 Message boards
We encourage users of the Website to contribute to our message boards, some of which are reserved for subscribers, and some of which are for general use. You must follow our Bulletin Board Rules of Conduct [LINK], and use is only authorized on that basis.

We expect many of those contributing to our message boards to have strong views about _____, but the Website is subject to the laws of libel, and you and we could be sued if you are not careful in what you say. You should not make libellous postings or any postings which are illegal or breach copyright, database or other related rights. It is your responsibility to check this out, and we do not accept any liability in this respect.

If you see any information on the Website which breaches your or anyone else's rights or may be illegal, defamatory or otherwise should be removed, let us know immediately and, where we agree, we shall do our best to remove it as soon as possible.

You must indemnify (pay) us for any losses we suffer if you breach this provision or any other provision of these Terms or the Bulletin Board Code of Conduct.

Although we listen to users' suggestions for new message boards, we cannot guarantee to include every topic everyone requests.

We reserve the right to remove postings to message boards or edit them at our discretion, but have no obligation to do so.

Some message boards have restricted access, and use is limited, for example, only to subscribers of EFG. To subscribe, click here [LINK].

Subscribers must ensure that only they use those message boards, and that they do not allow non-subscribers to use them using a subscriber's own password.

Subscribers must keep their passwords confidential.

5 Our liability

We provide information on this Website free of any access charge and on the basis of no liability for the information given.

In no event shall we be liable to you for any direct or indirect or consequential loss, loss of profit, revenue or goodwill arising from your use of the Website or information on the Website. All terms implied by law are excluded.

We accept liability for death or personal injury caused by negligence or responsibility for fraudulent misrepresentation that cannot, under English law, be excluded.

We are a distributor (and not a publisher) of content supplied by third parties and users of the Website. Any opinions, advice, statements, services, offers or other information or content expressed or made available by third parties, including information providers or users, are those of the authors or distributors, and not of us. We do not necessarily endorse nor are we responsible for the accuracy or reliability of any opinion, advice or statement made on the Website.

6 Barring from the Website

We reserve the right to bar users from the Website, whether they are EFG subscribers or not, on a permanent or temporary basis at our discretion. Any such user shall be notified, and must not then attempt to use the Website under any other name or through any other user.

7 Legal jurisdiction and dispute-resolution

English law shall apply to these terms, notwithstanding the jurisdiction where you are based. You irrevocably agree that the courts of England shall have exclusive jurisdiction to settle any dispute which may arise out of, under, or in connection with these Terms, and for those purposes irrevocably submit all disputes to the jurisdiction of the English courts. The place of performance shall be England.

8 General

Any formal legal notices should be sent to us at the address at the end of these Terms by e-mail confirmed by post.

Failure by us to enforce a right does not result in waiver of such right.

You may not assign or transfer your rights under this agreement.

Further information

Further information on these conditions or any queries on them can be obtained from:

The Legal Officer, EFG Limited, _____.
Telephone: (+44) (0) _____. Facsimile: (+44) (0) _____.
E-mail: <legal@efg.co.uk>.

EFG Limited is a company registered in England, registered office at _____.

**TERMS AND CONDITIONS FOR
USE OF WEBSITE <www.the-efg.co.uk>
AND CONTRIBUTIONS TO BULLETIN
BOARDS, Version 1, 1 May 2000**

SEPARATE NOTICE FOR BULLETIN BOARD PAGE

Rules of conduct

We encourage users of the <www.the-efg.co.uk> Website ('the Website') to contribute freely to our bulletin boards, as long as they do it responsibly, free of insult and respectful of others. To ensure you and we are protected, we have developed a standard of conduct that is strictly enforced. These Rules of Conduct should be read with our Terms and Conditions for Use of Website, which contain important information about our liability and copyright matters [LINK].

Comments posted on our message boards which violate our standards are routinely removed without further comment.

Our standards are:

- No profanity or obscenities of any kind, even disguised with *asterisks.
- No personal attacks on other participants (personal attacks are defined as comments that reflect upon the person, instead of their opinion).
- Slanderous, defamatory, obscene, indecent, lewd, pornographic, violent, abusive, insulting, threatening and harassing comments are not tolerated.
- Please do not stray from the discussion topic.
- No impersonation of other participants or public figures. A user may choose an appropriate nickname on message boards or in chat, as long as a real name is used in the personal information field (which is not publicly visible on the message side).
- No advertising of any kind, including non-profitmaking organizations.
- No third-party copyright material should be posted, although we encourage contributions to be sent for our Website. Please use links instead of quotes from sources, rather than copying the material.
- On message boards, no oversized fonts, JavaScript, tables, headings or other advanced HTML commands are allowed. Please use only bold or coloured fonts to emphasize your points.

End-user terms and conditions

Note: This is an example of terms and conditions to appear on a Website where users book services on the site and pay by credit card and the services are provided by various third parties who have contracted to make their services available via the ABC.com Website. The example also includes general provisions for use of a Website, copyright, data protection and related areas.

Websites differ widely. Specific legal advice should always be sought from specialist Internet lawyers. These conditions were drafted in 2000. There are many new ecommerce laws at UK and EU level currently being adopted. Up-to-date advice should always be obtained.

1 DEFINITIONS

In these Conditions, the following expressions shall have the following meanings:

The Website – <www.abc.com>: a Website through which ABC operates
TS – a supplier who provides [*services*] which can be booked through the
ABC Website
Booking – a Confirmed Reservation for which ABC has received a pay-
ment from a Client
User – someone who uses the ABC Website, whether they become a Client
or not
Client – an end-User buying services, usually acting through an employee
of the Client Company
ABC –ABC Ltd – A Company registered in England, No. ____ of ____
UK. Tel.: (+44) (0) ____. Fax: (+44) (0) ____; Website: <www.[abc].com>
Reservation – A ____ service reserved by the client online via ABC
Services – ____ services to be provided to the Client by TS and ABC

2 APPLICABLE TERMS

2.1   All bookings made through **ABC**, however made by any individual,
group or company, and all use of the **ABC** Website shall be subject to the
following terms and conditions. Users and Clients signify their acceptance
of these conditions by proceeding to use the Website and/or placing a
Booking. **ABC** may revise these terms and conditions at any time without
notice, at its discretion.

2.2   These terms shall be incorporated into all contracts, and in the case of
any inconsistency with any additional documentation between the parties to
the contract such as standard terms of **TS**, these conditions shall prevail as
between the Client and **ABC** unless explicitly varied in writing by a Director on behalf of **ABC**.

2.3   Clients placing a Booking, which is accepted by **ABC/TS**, form a
legally binding contract with **ABC** on the terms and conditions of this
agreement.

2.4   Where the individual placing the Booking is an employee or contractor of a company, the contract is with their employer, the Client. All individuals placing Bookings must ensure they have appropriate authority and
budget allocation for Bookings placed here, and are advised to check before
placing the Booking, as no cancellation on the grounds of lack of authority
is accepted.

2.5   **ABC** accept no liability for consequences arising out of unauthorized
behaviour by employee or agent of Client company.

3 AVAILABILITY

All reservations made on the **ABC** Website are accepted subject to availability. A Booking is confirmed once **ABC** has received payment in cleared funds.

4 FEES AND CHARGES

All fees and charges are payable in advance in the currency specified. No Booking will be accepted as final until payment is settled. Delegates will be unable to [*receive XYZ services*] booked with **ABC** unless payment is cleared beforehand. Value added or other sales tax will be added at the prevailing rates where applicable to all charges quoted.

Client will make bookings and payments to **ABC** at the online price on the Website, at the time of Booking, either by credit card, cheque or purchase order.

5 FORMATION OF CONTRACT FOR SERVICES PROVISION AND DUTIES

5.1   A contract is made between the Client and **ABC** on acceptance of a Booking. **ABC** reserves the right to reject any Booking put forward by a Client without reason at its discretion. **ABC** and **TS** cannot guarantee that all [*services*] advertised are available, and they reserve the right to substitute [*XYZ*].

5.2   Client undertakes to book only those services for which it has the technical capability to receive, and agrees not to misrepresent this.

5.3   Client shall complete a [*services*] review form and supply it to **ABC** after the services are provided, and **ABC** shall be entitled to use and copy for marketing and other purposes the information given on such form in any way at its discretion.

6 CANCELLATION

6.1   All [*services*], if booked as part of a 'special promotion', or with 'special discounts' arrangement, cannot be cancelled, and no refund will be made.

6.2   Subject to clause 6.1 above, [*services*] may be rescheduled by Clients without additional charge, provided **ABC** receives the request to reschedule in writing at least 15 working days before the services are to be performed, and further provided that a further similar or suitable such service provision is available. As a result of individual **TS** policies, later notification may result in partial or no refund being offered.

6.3   If the **TS** cancels or postpones the booking, **ABC** is absolved from any liability whatsoever except for the refund of fees already paid by the Client or rescheduling of the services. This is a matter outside **ABC**'s control, although it will use reasonable endeavours to notify Clients as soon as possible.

6.4   If the Client has any complaint or comment about the quality of content of the services after they are provided, this should be raised with **TS**, save to the extent that **ABC** welcomes feedback in its users' forum.

7   CONDITIONS AND WARRANTIES RELATING TO ABC WEBSITE

7.1   **ABC** Website may assist Clients in choosing services, but the assessment and selection of the Client's chosen [*services*] for the Client's purpose remains the Client's ultimate responsibility. **ABC** accepts no liability in this respect, and undertakes only that in giving such assistance it has acted in good faith and has not been wilfully misleading. In particular, but without limitation, **ABC** does not warrant that every [*example of the services publicly available*] is available on the Website.

7.2   The **TS** will at all times be responsible for ensuring that all schedules, prices and other information provided online on the **ABC** Website shall be accurate and up to date. **ABC** accepts no responsibility for any inaccurate information or misrepresentations made in the **TS** information. Any resulting loss or damage caused by reliance on **TS**'s information shall be the sole liability of **TS**. Clients or Users of the Site are strongly advised to take their own independent advice.

7.3   In no event shall **ABC** be liable to any Client or User of the Website or the information on the Website for any indirect or consequential loss, loss of profit, revenue or goodwill. **ABC**'s total liability shall be limited to the profit it makes on the Client/User concerned. Nothing in these terms shall exclude or limit **ABC**'s liability for death or personal injury caused by negligence, or its responsibility for fraudulent misrepresentation that cannot as a matter of English law be excluded.

7.4   **ABC** makes no warranty that all [*services*] on the Website are approved [*give services type here, and approvals body, if any*] by the [_____], but undertakes to use reasonable endeavours to specify which are approved and which are not.

8   FORCE MAJEURE

In the event of cancellations due to floods, terrorism, strikes, actions by the government or agencies acting on its behalf, or other natural and other factors outside the reasonable control of **ABC**, **ABC** and **TS** will attempt to reschedule the services or provide a refund of the fees to the Client. No further liability shall ensue.

9   LEGAL JURISDICTION AND DISPUTE-RESOLUTION

English law shall apply to these terms and the relationship with Clients and Users of the Website, notwithstanding the jurisdiction where the Client/User is based. The parties irrevocably agree that the courts of England shall have exclusive jurisdiction to settle any dispute which may arise out of, under, or in connection with these Terms or the legal relationship established by them, and for those purposes irrevocably submit all disputes to the jurisdiction of the English courts. The place of performance shall be England.

10   DISCLAIMER

10.1   Due to the number of sources from which **ABC** obtains content and the nature of electronic distribution via the World Wide Web, **ABC** does not give any warranties in respect of the Website. All implied warranties are excluded from these terms to the extent that they may be excluded as a matter of law.

10.2   **Year 2000**: Although the **ABC** Website is Y2K compliant, **ABC** makes no warranty that external online **TS** Websites are Y2K compliant or free from infection by viruses or anything else that has contaminating or destructive properties.

10.3   Clients/Users should retain copies of all data, which they send to or through the Website.

11 INTELLECTUAL PROPERTY RIGHTS, CONFIDENTIALITY AND DATA PROTECTION

11.1   All the content and images on the **ABC** Website are the property of **ABC**, the **TS** or their licensors, including without limitation all copyright and database rights in such works and the software underlying them and the trade marks and trade names used on the Website. All rights are reserved.

11.2   Clients/Users may print the information on the **ABC** Website and copy and e-mail it for the purpose of notifying others of the details on the Website, provided it is unaltered. However, the information must not be commercialized or used in any other Website without the prior written permission of **ABC**.

11.3   Clients and Users will indemnify and hold **ABC** and its employees and **TS**'s harmless against all loss and liability arising from claims made or litigation brought against them as a result of the use by the Client/User of the **ABC** Website's contents.

11.4   **Security: ABC** uses [*NetBanx's*] secure site for all Credit Card authorizations and transactions.

11.5   **Privacy policy: ABC**'s servers do not automatically record e-mail addresses. Domain names and IP addresses are aggregates solely for statistical purposes. Where a Client orders [*services*] or sends an e-mail to **ABC**, their personal data will be recorded and retained by **ABC** in accordance with the UK Data Protection Act 1998. Clients/Users agree that their data may be used by **ABC** or **TS** for further e-mail or other direct marketing purposes for goods or services in which they may be interested, and may be exported from the European Economic Area, including to jurisdictions where there are no data protection laws. Clients/Users who object to this should notify **ABC** and they will be removed from all mailing lists. **ABC** does not sell on personal data to third parties. Clients and Users clicking to indicate acceptance of these terms are giving their specific and explicit consent to all such uses/export of their personal data to the fullest extent permitted by law.

11.6   **Links**: Clients/Users do not need to request permission to create a text link with this Website. Those wishing to use a logo or graphics of **ABC** or a **TS**, however, must obtain prior written consent.

11.7 **Accessibility of Website**: Although **ABC** does its best to ensure that the Website is accessible, it cannot guarantee it will always be so, and does not accept any liability for such non-accessibility. Clients should retain details of **TS**'s telephone and fax numbers for direct contact to check particular details of the services booked.

11.8 **Users' forum**: Users contributing to the users' forum on the Website must not disseminate any illegal or commercially sensitive information or pirated software. Users are responsible for ensuring that nothing defamatory is transmitted, and **ABC** hereby notifies Users that it does not exercise any control over such information, and accepts no liability therefore. However, users discovering any such information on the forum should notify **ABC** immediately. In particular, Users should respect the laws of defamation in sending messages about service providers, fellow clients for the services and [*software*] vendors.

11.9 **Barring from Website**: **ABC** reserves the right to bar Users from the Website on a permanent or temporary basis at its discretion. Any such User shall be notified, and must not then attempt to use the Website under any other name or through any other User.

11.10 **Age Restriction**: No Bookings will be accepted on this Website from any person under the age of **18** years or the age of majority in the country in which they are resident.

11.11 **General**: Any formal legal notices should be sent to **ABC** at the address in paragraph 1 by e-mail confirmed by post. Failure by **ABC** to enforce a right does not result in waiver of such right. Clients accept they have not relied on any representation in making a Booking.

FURTHER INFORMATION

Further information on these conditions or any queries about them can be obtained from ABC.com Ltd, a company registered in England of ____ UK. Tel.: (+44) (0) ____. Fax: (+44) (0) ____. Website: <www.[abc].com>.

For more information, call free: 0800 ____.

NOTES (NOT PART OF THE CONTRACT)

The contract is merely an example of a Website set of conditions. No example should ever be used without appropriate modifications, depending on the circumstances, and ideally after taking advice from Internet lawyers.

Details of computer/IT/Internet lawyers are contained in the Chambers & Partners' Directory at: <http://www.chambersandpartners.com>.

Users would not be allowed to use the Website unless and until they had actively clicked to show acceptance of the conditions. When they 'click', they become parties to the agreement between the parties.

The Website is to allow users to book services offered by a variety of third-party providers, not the company, ABC, providing the Website. In other cases of direct supply, the conditions can be simplified. In this case, there would also need to be an agreement between the suppliers – TS – and ABC governing their own contractual relationship.

The contract specifically does not exclude the Contracts (Rights of Third Parties) Act 1999, but thought should always be given to this issue.

There would have been a contract with the company which designed the Website, ensuring that all intellectual property rights in the Website and its design are owned by the client – ABC in this example.

The Website has a privacy policy included in its conditions. Some Websites have a separate policy of this sort available in their site – such as that of the Information Commissioner on <http://www.dataprotection.gov.uk> or <http://www.dell.com>.

There may be other legal notices on the Website as well, such as a general copyright notice or notice about registered trade marks. These are not given here.

The Data Protection Act 1998 needs careful consideration. Although these conditions provide a consent from the user/client to their data being used for direct marketing and export from the EEA, this may not be sufficient for such consent to be specific and informed and to satisfy the UK Information Commissioner. Advice should be sought – see <http://www.dataprotection.gov.uk>, particularly as regards the Advice (2000) on export of data from the EEA.

The Website and its conditions are subject to English law. It specifically provides that the place of performance is in England because the draft EU regulation on jurisdiction likely to be agreed in 2000 provides that parties may specify their own place of performance in their contract.

Consumers may need different terms. The services purchased on this site are envisaged to be business services. In particular, unfair terms law and the Consumer Protection (Distance Selling) Regulations 2000 which implemented the distance selling directive 97/7 from 31 October 2000 in the UK, give special rights to consumers. Consumers may have rights to cancel, and certain terms may be challenged as unfair.

The general provisions at the end of the contract are likely to be of greater application than the specific provisions relating to the services concerned and bookings with third parties (TS) in practice.

APPENDIX 4 CONTRACT WITH SUB-CONTRACTOR/ DESIGNER

This is drafted from the point of view of the buyer of the services from the sub-contractor.

[Company name]

This document sets out the terms we have agreed for our use of your services for us. It forms a legal agreement between us [*Company name*] and you. Your details are set out on the attached Schedule.

1. You agree to provide the services to us described on the attached Schedule ('the Services').
2. We shall pay you the fees set out in the Schedule either by way of a monthly retainer payment or a fixed fee (see Schedule).
3. We will/will not reimburse your reasonable expenses agreed with us in writing in advance in arrears at the end of each month.
4. You may provide the Services either at your home, other premises or our premises at your discretion, save where we reasonably require you to perform the Services at our premises. Where you use our offices and wish to do so in addition for work for other clients of yours, you shall inform us in advance, and you may proceed unless we notify you that we object to this use of our resources.
5. All intellectual property rights, including without limitation copyright, in material produced by you in the course of performing the Services shall vest in us, and you agree to sign all documents necessary to ensure our ownership of those rights. You may only use such material in order to perform this Agreement, and may not, in particular but without limitation, use such material for other clients of yours. Where you have already supplied material to us, you hereby assign all intellectual property rights in such material to us.
6. You shall ensure that all copyright and other notices we require to appear shall appear on the material to be produced by you, and you will claim no intellectual property rights in such material.

7. You waive your moral rights in relation to material provided by you under this Agreement.

8. You will provide the Services for which you are contracted by the date/dates set out in the Schedule or otherwise agreed in writing with us. Time shall be of the essence under this clause.

9. You warrant that the material provided by you under this agreement is your own original work and does not infringe the intellectual property rights of any third party, is not defamatory, obscene, blasphemous or in breach of any law or regulation. You agree fully to indemnify us and hold us harmless from all costs, losses and expenses including legal fees arising from any breach of this warranty.

10. You shall ensure that work undertaken for us is given priority by you over other projects or work to be undertaken by you, and that you inform us in advance of any holiday or other absence plans which may interfere with the schedule agreed by us for performance of the Services.

11. The Services to be performed shall be carried out with due skill and care and in accordance with the highest standards of the industry and as set out in the Schedule.

12. You shall perform the Services personally. Where you are a limited company, you shall ensure that named individuals perform the Services, the names of which individuals we agree in advance.

13. Where computer software or tangible work product is supplied by you as part of the Services, it shall be of satisfactory quality and fit for the purpose agreed between us and otherwise in accordance with the description set out in the Schedule or other documentation agreed between us.

14. Your agreement with us is solely for the performance of the Services, and we do not undertake to offer you work on any future occasion or have a continuing obligation to utilize your services. You have informed us that you are self-employed, and therefore you are responsible for your own national insurance and tax payments. Where you are registered for Value Added Tax, you set out your registration number in the Schedule. You are required to work the hours necessary to perform the Services at your discretion in accordance with this agreement. No relationship of employer and employee is contained in these terms.

15. We reserve the right to terminate our contract with you on one month's notice in writing sent to our address above notwithstanding that all the work in relation to the Services has not been completed by you.

16. On termination or expiry of this agreement, you shall return to us all documents, information, software or other property of ours and cease to use such materials, and shall not retain any copies in any format.

17. You will keep our confidential information strictly confidential and only use it for the purposes of performing this agreement.

18. For the duration of this Agreement you shall not become involved in competitive projects. You will notify us in advance of your current projects/work for clients so we can determine whether such projects are competitive and may preclude your performing the Services.

19. No variation of this Agreement will be valid unless agreed in writing by us both.

20. You may not assign this Agreement without our prior written consent.

21. This Agreement sets out the entire Agreement between us save for any confidentiality agreement between us or other documents referred to in the Schedule.

22. If any provision of this Agreement is found to be invalid or unenforceable, such invalidity or unenforceability shall not affect the other provisions of this Agreement, all of which shall remain in full force and effect.

23. If we are slow to enforce our rights or do not do so, we may still do so in future.

24. All notices shall be in writing and sent to the address of the recipient set out above or such other address as the recipient may designate by notice given in accordance with this provision. Any notice may be delivered personally by first class pre-paid letter or facsimile transmission (confirmed by first-class post) and shall be deemed to have been served if by personal delivery when delivered, if by first-class post 48 hours after posting, and if by facsimile transmission when despatched (with successful transmission report).

25. This Agreement shall be governed by English law, and we both submit to the non-exclusive jurisdiction of the English courts in relation to any dispute under this Agreement.

26. No right is given by this agreement to any third party, and the Contracts (Rights of Third Parties) Act 1999 shall not apply.

Please confirm your acceptance of these terms by signing below.

Signed by Subcontractor:

———

In the presence of:

———

Witness

We, the Buyer, agree to the above terms

Signed by:

In the presence of:

Witness

The schedule

1. Your name
2. Your business address and registered company number, where relevant
3. Your VAT registration number, where relevant
4. Description of the Services to be provided
5. Date of commencement of contract
6. Fees – monthly retainer/fixed fee
7. Delivery date(s).

INDEX

Directors' Duties and Liabilities

Paul J. Omar

The law relating to directors' duties has fundamental implications across the business environment and yet few areas of business law have received so little detailed examination. This text provides fresh and incisive insights to the rules applying in ten major economic jurisdictions within Europe, with respect to directors' legal obligations and liabilities. Written by the foremost figures in the field, each contribution outlines the statutory provisions that affect the work of company directors in each jurisdiction, including general legislation and specific laws covering the status of incorporated bodies. Fully illustrated with case-law examples the book provides a guide to the range of measures which national courts may provide for participants in corporate life seeking remedies for unsatisfactory governance of companies. It also features guidance on the specific bases for criminal and civil liabilities and examples of the range of penalties to which directors might be subject. The result is a work of unprecedented detail which will be welcomed by practitioners in the corporate sector, academics and researchers alike.

GOWER

Contract Negotiation Handbook

Third Edition

P.D.V. Marsh

Every organization enters into agreements for purchase and supply of goods
and services, and most managers have some involvement in negotiating.
Moreover the successful planning, execution and conclusion of contract
negotiations can contribute directly to corporate profitability.

The CONTRACT NEGOTIATION HANDBOOK explains how the need to negotiate arises
and how to form a negotiating plan. It sets out a structured approach
to negotiation through all its various stages – preparing to negotiate,
the opening of negotiations and how these develop at the negotiating table,
and the closing and recording of the bargain. The use and misuse of certain
tactics in negotiation are also covered.

This classic text has now been thoroughly updated and revised, employing
a more user-friendly approach. New features include a discussion of partnering
and the importance of long-term relationships and contracts. The role of the
psychology of bargaining is integrated throughout the text, rather than being
treated as a separate entity.

GOWER

Getting Out of a Contract – A Practical Guide for Business

Adam Rose, David Leibowitz and Adrian Magnus

This book is written by three commercial lawyers. Their clients often ask them as much for help in getting out of a contract as in getting them into one in the first place. Built around two business case studies, the book highlights the various legal issues that a business must address when faced with a contract it wants to walk away from. In the first instance the business needs to discover whether it is as shackled by a contract as it thinks it is. In many cases a contract is not as binding as it might initially appear – GETTING OUT OF A CONTRACT explains the circumstances in which this applies. It then goes on to explore how to minimize the damage should the agreement be inescapable and helps the reader to understand what the consequences of any actions might be.

Written in plain English, the authors manage to demystify complicated aspects of English law for the non-lawyer. This book will help managers to:

• address how they make contracts;
• avoid making wrong decisions because they fail to appreciate what contracts they actually have or how to get round them;
• become more attuned to the legal ins and outs of contracts, enabling them to use lawyers more cost-effectively

Company secretaries, finance directors and managers at all levels will find GETTING OUT OF A CONTRACT accessible and an invaluable business planning tool.

GOWER

The Outsourcing R&D Toolkit

Outsourcing Research and Development Toolkit

Peter Sammons

Research and Development (R&D) is a key 'factor of production' in the global business environment and yet there can be no doubt that research budgets are under attack as never before. International competitive pressure means that companies, and countries, must innovate or die even though funding is often decreasing. The answer to this dichotomy is to ensure better value for money – and this toolkit will lead you towards that goal.

THE OUTSOURCING R&D TOOLKIT comprehensively covers the strategic and tactical issues necessary for a company to decide whether, and to what extent, to buy in their knowledge-based services. Having done this it then goes on to provide a toolbox of commercial materials to enable better control of external R&D projects. It consists of two main parts:

• *Part I: Buying Research Services* – this provides an up-to-date briefing on contract R&D, practices, procedures and pitfalls. It includes 70+ learning points which highlight issues particularly important to companies buying-in R&D services.
• *Part II: Contract Research Toolbox* of template contract and contract management documents including instructions for use: these materials are subtly tailored to the commercial interests of the knowledge buyer and form a contracting system in their own right. Use these to benchmark existing company practices and procedures.

Buying in R&D services is undoubtedly the way of the future and a core management competence across all industrial sectors. THE OUTSOURCING R&D TOOLKIT will stop you from being left behind!

GOWER